American Bar Association
Section of International Law and Practice
Committee on Comparative Procedure and Practice

Harold H. Healy, Jr. - Co-Chairman
Lyon L. Brinsmade
Paul B. Hannon
Harry A. Inman

Sydney M. Cone, III - Co-Chairman
M. Sean McMillan
Martin Perlberger
John H. Riggs, Jr.

The Regulation of Foreign Lawyers

(Third Edition)

by Sydney M. Cone, III

Library of Congress Catalog Card No. 84-72263

ISBN 0-89707-155-7

August 1, 1984

The Regulation of Foreign Lawyers

The Regulation of Foreign Lawyers

Introduction

The first edition of this work appeared in 1977, the second edition in 1980. In each case the available copies were sold rather rapidly. As a result, the material has been updated and expanded, and this third edition has been prepared.

The following material is divided into two sections. Section I briefly describes the rules affecting lawyers from other nations seeking to establish themselves and to practice on a regular basis in eleven jurisdictions in the United States. (The legal profession in the United States is regulated by the individual states; nevertheless, all of the states are obligated to follow In re Griffiths,[1] in which the United States Supreme Court found that, under the Constitution of the United States, a state may not deny admission to the Bar solely on grounds of citizenship.) Section II briefly describes the rules governing American lawyers in six jurisdictions within the European Community ("EC") (Belgium, England, France, Germany, Italy, Netherlands); in the EC as such; and in Australia, Brazil, Canada, China, Hong Kong, Israel, Japan, Mexico, Nigeria and Singapore.

The following material mainly involves lawyers seeking to establish themselves and to practice in a particular jurisdiction on a regular

---

[1] 413 U.S. 717 (1973).

basis, and generally does not deal with rules permitting a lawyer from another jurisdiction to render legal services on a temporary basis (e.g., by appearing specially in connection with a particular case). In addition, the following material does not attempt to take into account either (1) the extent to which ultimate decisions on the admission or licensing of individual applicants in a particular jurisdiction may come within the discretion of administrative, judicial or rule-making authorities or (2) the extent to which professional activities of a legal nature may be tolerated notwithstanding the formal rules in a given jurisdiction.

A number of lawyers have provided invaluable assistance in the preparation of this material, including E. Anthony Zaloom (California), John L. Bonee, III (Connecticut), Laurel A. Nichols (Florida), Thomas L. Nicholson (Illinois), William C. Benjamin (Massachusetts), Frederick J. Dennehy of Wilentz, Goldman & Spitzer (New Jersey), Herbert J. Hansell (Ohio), Andrew N. Farley (Pennsylvania), Mont P. Hoyt (Texas), Anthony G. Bancroft (Australia), William B. Meissner (Brazil), Micheline A. Filion (Canada), Sally A. Harpole (China), Mark H. Sheldon (England), Mendel Shapiro (Israel), Alexander C. Hoagland, Jr. and José Luis Siquieros (Mexico) and Maxwell O. Chibundu (Nigeria). Henry C. Schmeltzer and Diane Winters have contributed to the editing and preparation of this material.

I. Regulation of Foreign Lawyers in Eleven United States Jurisdictions.

Summary

Of the eleven jurisdictions covered in this section, only New York has adopted special rules for the licensing of legal consultants who have not taken an American bar examination. Under these New York rules, qualified lawyers who have been admitted and have practiced abroad can be licensed to carry on a consulting practice in New York. In addition, New York has adopted a special rule for the foreign-educated lawyer who wishes to take the New York bar examination and become a full-fledged member of the Bar.

In Massachusetts, the Board of Bar Examiners has discretionary authority to admit to the Bar, without examination, a foreign lawyer who has practiced or taught law for at least five years.

In Ohio, a foreign-educated lawyer may take the bar examination upon favorable evaluation of the applicant's educational qualifications by the Supreme Court of that state.

In the District of Columbia and in Pennsylvania, there are rules enabling a foreign lawyer to take the bar examination after attending an American law school for one year.

In Connecticut, "an alien lawfully residing in the United States" who meets the other qualifications for admission may apply for admission to the Bar.

In Texas, the Board of Law Examiners has discretionary authority to allow a "resident alien" to take the bar examination.

In New Jersey, foreign applicants for admission may take the bar examination after meeting requisite educational requirements.

Florida has adopted special rules to permit Cuban-Americans to take the bar examination.

New York has special rules for the admission to the Bar, without examination, of applicants who have practiced in a jurisdiction where the jurisprudence is based on English Common Law. Illinois, however, no longer has a similar rule. California waives its law student's examination, but not its bar examination or attorneys' examination, for practitioners from such an English Common Law jurisdiction and, in some cases, for practitioners from other foreign jurisdictions.

Analysis by Jurisdiction

California

The Business and Professions Code of California[1] requires that a person admitted as an attorney in California (in addition to being at least 18 years of age and of good moral character) must have completed, before beginning the study of law, at least two years of college work constituting at least half of the work acceptable for a bachelor's degree at a college or university approved by the examining committee.[2] A showing that the individual has "attained in apparent intellectual ability the equivalent of at least two years of the college work" described above can also satisfy the pre-legal education requirements if the applicant meets this standard to the satisfaction of a law school, accredited by the examining committee, where the applicant applies for admission. If the applicant is not applying for admission to an accredited law school, determination of the requisite intellectual ability may instead be made by the examining committee itself after a personal interview, or the examining committee may require the applicant to pass a written examination given by the examining committee or, if it so elects, under its supervision "by such members of the faculty of a college as the examining committee may select or by the [California] Department of Education." The examination

---

1 Cal. Bus. & Prof. Code § 6060 (West Supp. 1979).

2 *Id.* §§ 6060(a), (b), (c)(1).

must be successfully completed prior to the commencement of studying law.[3]

The legal education requirement for admission to the California Bar is satisfied by graduation from a law school accredited by the examining committee, but it also may be satisfied by alternative methods of study, including correspondence courses "requiring 864 hours of preparation and study per year for four years," study for four years under the supervision of a judge of a court of record or other member of the Bar or study for four years at a law school "that is authorized to confer professional degrees and requires classroom attendance of its students for a minimum of 270 hours a year."[4] No reported cases construe the latter alternative as it relates to schools located outside the United States.

Further prerequisites to admission are successful completion of the bar examination as well as a "first-year law student's examination." The latter requirement applies to all persons attending schools other than those accredited by the examining committee, except those applicants who have "passed the bar examination of a sister state or of a country wherein the common law of England constitutes the basis of jurisprudence." No credit is given for any law studies until the first-year law student's examination is successfully completed, at which time only one year of credit

---

[3] Id. § 6060(c)(2).

[4] Id. § 6060(e). The four years' study under a member of the Bar must be under the personal supervision of a person who is and for at least five years has continuously been practicing law.

is allowed, "unless for good cause in a particular case the committee decides that credit should be given" for studies completed subsequent to the first year of law school.[5]

Section 6062 of the Business and Professions Code and the rules promulgated pursuant thereto provide that an "out-of-state" attorney may be certified for admission to practice law in California if (in addition to being at least 18 years of age and of good moral character) the attorney has been admitted to practice "before the highest court of a sister state or of any foreign state or country" and has been "actively and substantially engaged in the practice of law" for four of the six years immediately preceding the application for admission, or has "demonstrated to the satisfaction of the examining committee that his experience and qualifications qualify him to take an examination." In addition, the applicant must pass either the bar examination or such other examination (called the "attorneys' examination") "as in the discretion of the examining committee may be required."[6]

An attorney applicant who is over 18 years of age, of good moral character and admitted to practice before the highest court of any state or other jurisdiction "where the common law of England constitutes the basis of jurisprudence," may be certified for admission to the Bar upon satisfying the committee "that his or her experience and qualifica-

---

[5] Id. § 6060(g); foll. § 6069, Rule IX.

[6] Id. § 6062.

tions qualify him or her to take the final bar examination and he or she has passed the final bar examination."[7] The countries included within this rule are Australia, Canada, India, Irish Republic, New Zealand, Pakistan, Republic of the Philippines, Republic of South Africa, Zimbabwe and the United Kingdom of Great Britain and Northern Ireland.[8] Applicants from other non-U.S. jurisdictions "have the burden of establishing to the satisfaction of the committee that the common law of England constitutes the basis of jurisprudence in such jurisdiction."[9] Attorneys from non-English Common Law jurisdictions, who are otherwise qualified, may be certified for admission upon passing the bar examination.[10] In order to qualify for admission to the bar examination, however, such an applicant must first "establish that he or she has adequate preparation in the fundamental principles of law examined on in the final bar examination and that the extent and quality of his or her pre-legal and legal training by formal education or experience or a combination of the two, is substantially equivalent to that required under [the rules covering legal or pre-legal educational requirements]."[11]

In October 1976, the Board of Governors of the State Bar of California, following a recommendation of its Committee on Unauthorized

---

[7] Id. foll. § 6069, Rule IV § 42(a)(3).

[8] Id. § 44(a).

[9] Id. § 44(b).

[10] Id. § 43(a)(4).

[11] Id. § 43(b).

Practice of Law, adopted a resolution disapproving any rule which would authorize "lawyers admitted in a foreign jurisdiction, but not in California, . . . to provide any legal services directly to members of the public in California."[12] It appears, however, that both the Board and that committee were acting after consideration of a proposal sponsored primarily by lawyers licensed in other countries who had been residing for some time in California; as reflected in their proposal, those lawyers were most interested in representing fellow members of their immigrant communities in such "local" matters as lower court appearances and family relations.[13] In 1983, the Board of Governors began consideration of another proposal for the licensing in California of legal consultants from foreign countries, modeled on the rules governing such licensing currently in effect in New York.[14] As of February 1984, no conclusion had been reached on that proposal.

---

[12] Minutes of the Board of Governors of the State Bar of California § 11(c)(ii) (October 1976). See State Bar of California, Committee on Unauthorized Practice of Law, Report Regarding "Legal Consultants" (Oct. 13, 1976).

[13] Id. See also correspondence from Anthony Murray, President of the State Bar of California, to Mr. Shunji Higuchi, Secretary-General of the Japan Federation of Bar Associations (Nov. 11, 1982).

[14] See Memorandum from Robert D. Raven, Chairman of the Special Committee on Japanese Practice, to the Board of Governors of the California State Bar (Sept. 28, 1983).

Connecticut

In Connecticut, under the applicable Superior Court Rules and under the Bar Examining Committee Regulations,[1] an applicant must either (1) have received a bachelor of laws or equivalent degree from a law school "approved" by the Bar Examining Committee; or (2) after completing a bachelor of laws or equivalent degree "for work acceptable to the committee," have obtained a master of laws degree for "postgraduate work acceptable to the committee" at a law school "approved" by the Committee.[2] An "approved" law school means either a school approved by the American Bar Association ("ABA") or a member of the Association of American Law Schools.[3] In the case of an applicant who has obtained only a master of laws degree at an "approved" law school, the Committee makes its determinations case-by-case.

The applicant must be a citizen of the United States or "an alien lawfully residing in the United States."[4] Further, the applicant (in addition to being 18 years of age and of good moral character) must be a

---

1 Connecticut Practice Book § 8, et seq.; Regulations of the Connecticut Bar Examining Committee Regulating Admission to the Bar (State Bar Examining Committee Publication, 1984 edition).

2 Connecticut Practice Book § 16 (Fifth).

3 Connecticut Regulations, Article III.

4 Connecticut Practice Book § 16 (First). Connecticut has abolished its reciprocity requirement to the effect that an alien applicant must be a citizen of a country which permits United States citizens to become members of the Bar of that country. See id.

Connecticut state resident or must become a state resident prior to being admitted to the Bar.[5]

The applicant who meets the foregoing requirements must either pass the bar examination or else be eligible for admission without examination. Eligibility for admission without examination is limited to persons who, among other things, have actually practiced law in other United States jurisdictions for at least five years.[6] There are no procedures in Connecticut for admission of non-U.S. attorneys based on prior admission in jurisdictions outside the U.S.

---

[5] Id. § 16 (Second), (Third), (Fourth). The residency requirement is being tested in both federal and state court, and it may be modified in the near future. See Solomon v. Standing Committee on Recommendations for Admission for the Bar for New Haven County, Fed. Civ. Doc. N79-58; In re Admission to the Bar of John White, No. 288445 (Superior Court for the Hartford Judicial District, N. O'Neil, Judge).

[6] Id. § 21. For a definition of "actually practiced law" see In Re Application of Slade, 169 Conn. 677 (1975).

District of Columbia

In respect of an applicant who meets the general requirements of character and fitness,[1] the Rules of the District of Columbia Court of Appeals contain two provisions for admission to the Bar. First, an applicant who has graduated from a law school not approved by the American Bar Association and who has received credit for 24 hours of study in the subjects tested in the bar examination at an ABA-approved law school[2] may be admitted to the Bar if he or she has passed both the D.C. bar examination and an examination on the Code of Professional Responsibility given under the auspices of the Multistate Bar Examination Committee of the National Conference of Bar Examiners. Thus, an applicant for admission to the D.C. Bar who first attended a non-U.S. law school and who later obtained 24 hours of credit for courses in the United States (as through a year of studies for a master of laws degree) would be eligible to take the D.C. bar examination and, upon passing it, to gain full admission to the D.C. Bar.

Second, admission to the D.C. Bar without passing the D.C. bar examination is available to an attorney who is a member of a Bar of a court of general jurisdiction of any state or territory of the United States and who either (a) has practiced law on a full-time basis within the

---

[1] D.C. Cir. Rules § 46.I.(d).

[2] Id. §§ 46.I.(b)(3), (4).

United States for not less than five of the previous eight years or (b) is from a state or territory which could afford to a similarly qualified member of the D.C. Bar a reciprocal right of admission without examination.[3]

Lawyers who are only members of a foreign (non-U.S.) Bar apparently are ineligible for admission without examination. A proposal to license such lawyers to carry on a consulting practice in the District of Columbia is being considered by the D.C. Bar.

---

[3] Id. § 46.I.(c)(3).

Florida

Under the Rules of the Supreme Court of Florida, an applicant for admission to the Florida Bar must produce "satisfactory evidence to the Board [of Bar Examiners] of good moral character and an adequate knowledge of the standards and ideals of the profession and that such person is otherwise fit to take the oath and perform the obligations and responsibilities of an attorney."[1] Each applicant must be at least 18 years old, must meet specific pre-legal and legal educational requirements in order to become eligible to take the Florida bar examination and must successfully complete the examination.

Pre-legal educational requirements for those enrolling in law school after December 31, 1975 include receipt of an academic bachelor's degree on the basis of a four-year period of study in an accredited college or university. The requirement for those entering law school before December 31, 1960 is at least two years in-residence undergraduate work; it is three years for those enrolling between December 31, 1960 and December 31, 1975. All pre-legal educational requirements can be fulfilled by successful completion of an equivalency examination or, in the case of those enrolling in law school after December 31, 1975, by determination by a credentials evaluation service or other Board-approved professionals that the applicant's education is the equivalent of a bachelor's degree.[2]

---

[1] Fla. R. Ct., Rules of the Supreme Court Relating to Admissions to the Bar, Article III, § 2.

[2] Id., Article III, § 1(a).

Satisfactory evidence of graduation (or pending graduation) from a full-time ABA-accredited law school is a further requirement for admission.[3] The only waiver of this requirement relates to a special program for Cuban-Americans. By order of the Florida Supreme Court, dated July 31, 1973, an applicant is considered qualified for admission to the Florida bar examination and, upon its successful completion, for admission to the Florida Bar if, *inter alia*, the applicant "is an American citizen and bona fide resident of the State of Florida, who, prior to December 31, 1960, practiced law in Cuba and was a graduate of any of the following law schools: A. University of Habana (Havana); B. Jose Marti University; C. St. Thomas of Villanova Law School; D. Ceriente University." Each applicant, in addition to furnishing various documents supporting these requirements of the Court's Order, must attend an accredited law school in the State of Florida and successfully complete one year in residence.[4]

As an additional exception to the specific education requirements, the Florida rules provide that an applicant who does not meet the requirements as to pre-legal and/or legal education may, in the Board's discretion, be permitted to take the bar examination if such applicant is in good standing at the Bar of another U.S. jurisdiction and has been

---

3 *Id.*, Article III, § 1(b).

4 Order of the Florida Supreme Court, Case No. 43,040 (July 31, 1973).

practicing law in such jurisdiction for at least ten years and if the applicant presents an abstract containing samples of his or her work during the preceding ten years to illustrate to the Board's satisfaction that the applicant's "academic and legal scholarship conform to approved standards and sum up to the equivalent of that required of other applicants for admission to the Florida Bar Examination."[5]

The bar examination consists of one part that is a combination of essay and multiple-choice questions, one part that is the Multistate Bar Examination and a third part that is the Multistate Professional Responsibility Examination (covering ethics).

---

5 Fla. R. Ct., Rules of the Supreme Court Relating to Admissions to the Bar, Article III, § 1(c).

Illinois

Applicants for admission to practice law in Illinois must be 21 years of age and of good moral character, must have either satisfactorily passed the bar examination or (as discussed below) have been licensed to practice law in another U.S. jurisdiction, and (as discussed below) must have satisfactorily completed a professional responsibility examination.[1] Applicants for admission without taking the bar examination must also establish actual residence in Illinois and the intention of continuous and active practice of law.[2]

In order to take the bar examination, the applicant must have the requisite academic qualifications, which include the completion of high school and 90 semester hours at a college approved by the Board of Law Examiners. "In lieu of such preliminary or college work, the board may, after due investigation, accept the satisfactory completion of the program or curriculum of a particular college or university."[3] The legal education requirement is less flexible; the applicant must "within the period of six years immediately prior to making application . . . have pursued a course of law studies and fulfilled the requirements and received a first degree in law from a law school approved by the American Bar Association."[4]

---

1 Ill. Ann. Stat. ch. 110A § 701 (Smith-Hurd Supp. 1981).

2 Id. § 705(d).

3 Id. § 703(a) (Smith-Hurd 1976).

4 Id. § 703(b) (Smith-Hurd 1979).

The Illinois Supreme Court has granted very few, if any, petitions for a waiver of this rule for individual foreign-educated lawyers. In addition, the applicant must satisfactorily complete either a professional responsibility examination conducted by the Board of Law Examiners on the basis of the Illinois Code of Professional Responsibility or the Multistate Professional Responsibility Examination (this requirement has been in effect since July 1, 1981).

A procedure for admission on the basis of academic qualification without taking the bar examination is available for lawyers admitted to practice in the highest court of any U.S. jurisdiction, if the applicant meets the education requirements described above and "has resided and actively and continuously practiced law in such other jurisdiction for a period of at least five years of the seven years immediately prior to making the application" in Illinois. The requirement of a professional responsibility examination may be met by proving "to the satisfaction of the Board of Law Examiners" that the applicant "has written and scored a passing grade (as determined by the Board) in the Multistate Professional Responsibility Examination of the National Conference of Bar Examiners within five years prior to the date of the application." There is no longer a provision for the admission of lawyers from foreign countries without taking the bar examination.[5]

---

[5] Id. § 705 (Smith-Hurd Supp. 1981).

The Illinois Supreme Court has decided against adopting a proposal to license legal consultants from foreign countries. The first draft of the proposed rule was published in June 1975, and a revised version, which appeared in November 1975, was approved by the Board of Governors of the Illinois Bar Association on February 21, 1976.[6] Had it been adopted, the revised draft would have authorized the licensing of an individual admitted to practice as an attorney (or the equivalent) in another country to practice as a legal consultant without examination if the person (1) had "resided and actively and continuously practiced law in such other country" for at least three of the previous five years and had educational qualifications that would entitle him or her to take the bar examination in Illinois, or (2) had "actively and continuously practiced law in such other country" for at least five of the previous seven years. In addition, the proposal would have required that each applicant be an "actual resident" of Illinois who maintained or intended to maintain an office in the state for the continuous and active practice of foreign and international law.

Under the proposal, restrictions on the practice of legal consultants would have forbidden appearances before the state courts and preparation of pleadings and other documents relating to marital relations, child custody or disposition of property where a U.S. resident or citizen

---

6 Illinois State Bar Assoc., The Globe, Nos. 3, 4, 5 (June 1975, Nov. 1975, Dec. 1976).

was involved. Moreover, the licensed consultant could have advised on other aspects of U.S. law (either State or Federal) only on the basis of "advice from a person duly qualified and entitled" to render such advice.

Massachusetts

The general rules of the Supreme Judicial Court of Massachusetts entitled "Attorneys," as amended through December 21, 1982, provide in Section 3, entitled "Qualifications for Taking Bar Examination," that each applicant shall have graduated from high school and college, or shall "have received an equivalent education, in the opinion of the Board [of Bar Examiners]." Graduation from an ABA-approved law school, or a law school authorized to grant a bachelor of laws or juris doctor in Massachusetts, is also required.[1]

An applicant who was educated at a law school outside of the U.S., who satisfies the pre-legal educational requirements and whose legal education is considered by the Board to be equivalent to that provided in American law schools, may be permitted to take the bar examination. The Board may condition such permission upon designated further legal studies at an ABA-approved law school.[2]

Applicants who pass the bar examination and the Multistate Professional Responsibility Examination and "are found by the Board of Bar Examiners to be of good moral character" are eligible for admission "upon subscription to the attorney's oaths."[3]

---

1 Massachusetts Board of Bar Examiners, Information Relating to Admission of Attorneys in Massachusetts § 3 (1983).

2 Id. § 3.4.

3 Id. § 5.1.

The Massachusetts rules also provide that, in the discretion of the Board of Bar Examiners, attorneys admitted before the highest judicial court of a foreign country may be admitted to the Massachusetts Bar without examination if: (1) the applicant's "principal residence" is in Massachusetts; (2) the applicant has been "admitted in the foreign country for at least five years prior to applying for admission" and provides a certificate of such admission; (3) the applicant's pre-legal and legal education is equivalent to an American high school diploma, a college or university bachelor's degree and a bachelor of laws or juris doctor from a law school approved by the American Bar Association;[4] (4) the applicant has "engaged in the practice or teaching of law since the prior admission" so as to satisfy the Board of Bar Examiners "of his or her good moral character and professional qualifications"; (5) the applicant submits to the Board of Bar Examiners three letters of recommendation from attorneys in the foreign jurisdiction and two from Massachusetts attorneys; and (6) the applicant shall have passed the Multistate Professional Responsibility Examination.[5]

---

4 The rules contemplate recognition by the Board of Bar Examiners of "equivalent" foreign legal education; however, according to a letter from the Chairman of the Board of Bar Examiners dated November 19, 1982, the Board currently requires that a lawyer educated in a foreign country who is not admitted to the Bar of any other state of the United States secure a degree of juris doctor from an ABA-approved law school.

5 _Id._ § 6.2.

New Jersey

In New Jersey, under the Rules Governing the Courts of the State of New Jersey, as amended to September 12, 1983,[1] no person shall be admitted to the Bar of the State of New Jersey unless he or she shall have (1) passed the bar examination; (2) received a certification of good character by the Committee on Character; (3) attained a qualifying score on the Multistate Professional Responsibility Examination or passage of an approved course on professional ethics given by an American Bar Association-accredited law school; and (4) completed the required Skills and Methods course.[2] In order to be qualified for admission to the bar examination, a person must (a) prove that he is more than 18 years of age; (b) present a certification by a duly authorized officer of his law school that it is approved by the American Bar Association and that it has awarded him a bachelor of laws degree or its equivalent; and (c) present satisfactory evidence that he is a member of the Bar in good standing in every other jurisdiction in which he was ever admitted to practice.[3]

The Rule establishing qualification for admission to the bar examination was amended in 1973, in response to In re Griffiths, 413 U.S. 717 (1973), to eliminate its original requirement that the applicant be a

---

1 Rules Governing the Courts of the State of New Jersey (Sept. 12, 1983).

2 Id. Rule 1:27-1.

3 Id. Rule 1:24-2.

United States citizen.[4] The Rule was again amended to delete the requirement that the candidate be domiciled in New Jersey or certify his intention to establish within the state his domicile or principal office for the practice of law.[5] As the Rules now stand, an individual who is neither a U.S. citizen nor a permanent resident alien may be qualified to take the bar examination.

It should be noted that, although residency requirements for the taking of the bar examination have been abolished, no person holding a plenary license to practice in New Jersey is entitled to practice there unless he maintains a bona fide office for the practice of law in New Jersey, regardless of where he is domiciled.[6] A "bona fide office" is defined as a place where the attorney or a person acting on his behalf can be reached in person and by telephone during normal business hours.[7]

There is one exception to the requirement that an applicant for admission to practice in New Jersey pass the bar examination and complete the Skills and Methods course. This exception applies to an applicant, otherwise qualified, who has been domiciled in New Jersey, who has en-

---

4 Citzenship was required for admission to the examination prior to September 19, 1973 under former Rule 1:24-2(a).

5 These requirements were set forth in Rule 1:24-2(e) prior to September 11, 1978 and in Rule 1:24-2(d) from September 11, 1978 to September 1981.

6 Rule 1:21-1(a)

7 Id.

gaged on a full-time basis in teaching law at an approved law school in New Jersey for five years immediately preceding his application, and who has been admitted as an attorney of another state whose educational qualifications for admission to the Bar are equal to those of New Jersey.[8]

[8] Rule 1:27-2

New York

A number of foreign attorneys have been admitted to the New York Bar, either after passing the bar examination or after successfully applying for admission without taking the examination. In addition, under separate judicial rules, a number of foreign lawyers have been licensed as legal consultants in New York. Finally, a few foreign law firms, without seeking to have a lawyer either admitted to the New York Bar or licensed as a legal consultant, have established offices in New York for the limited purpose of giving advice to local lawyers in private practice or in the legal departments of corporations or institutions, but not to the general public.

Admission to the Bar

A foreign citizen is entitled to seek admission to the New York Bar on an equal footing with U.S. citizens, either by passing the New York bar examination or by complying with the requirements for admission without examination.[1] The applicant need not be a resident of New York but, possibly, must be a resident of the United States.[2]

---

1 Rules of the New York Court of Appeals for the Admission of Attorneys and Counselors at Law, [1983] 22 N.Y.C.R.R. Part 520 (hereinafter the "N.Y. Rules").

2 Prior to January 1, 1980, an applicant to take the New York bar examination was required to reside, or to intend to reside, in New York for at least six months. [1979] 22 N.Y.C.R.R. § 520.2(a)(3). Following In re Gordon, 48 N.Y.2d 266 (1979) (resident of North Carolina may not be constitutionally excluded from New York Bar solely because of nonresidency in New York), this requirement was deleted in its entirety, and no residency requirement for admission to the Bar is found in the N.Y. Rules. In re Gordon did not, however, involve an applicant residing outside the United States. While (Footnote continued)

Admission to the Bar - Bar Examination

To qualify to take the New York bar examination, an applicant must be over 21 years of age and must comply with one of three sections in the N.Y. Rules: (1) the section which deals with obtaining "a first degree in law" from an "approved law school"; or (2) the section on studying law in the office of a practicing attorney following the successful completion of at least one year's study at an "approved law school"; or (3) the section governing "an applicant who has studied in a foreign country."[3]

An applicant who has obtained "a first degree in law" from an "approved law school" (or who has studied law in the office of a practicing attorney) must have "commenced the study of law" after the applicant's 18th birthday.[4] The N.Y. Rules define an "approved law school" as one which (a) meets requirements specified in the N.Y. Rules and (b) is approved by the ABA or is a member of the Association of American Law Schools or is registered and approved by the New York State Education Department.[5]

---

that case does not expressly deal with foreign citizens, the N.Y. Rules seem to make no distinctions on the basis of citizenship as regards residency in New York.

3 N.Y. Rules § 520.2(a)(3); §§ 520.3, 520.4, 520.5.

4 Id. §§ 520.3(a)(1), 520.4(a)(1).

5 Id. §§ 520.3(b)-(h). In this connection an "approved law school" is permitted to "allow such credit as it may determine . . . to an applicant who studied in a law school in a foreign country." Id. § 520.3(i).

A provision of the N.Y. Rules entitled "Study of Law in Foreign Country; Required Legal Education" came into effect on January 1, 1980 and sets forth the requirements for an applicant who has studied law in a foreign country and who intends to take the New York bar examination.[6] Proof of compliance with this provision has been put under the jurisdiction of the New York State Board of Law Examiners.[7]

As to legal education, the applicant who studied law in another country is required to have completed "the educational requirements for admission to the practice of law" in that country. In fulfilling this requirement, the applicant, in a law school "recognized by the competent accrediting agency of the government of such other country," must have completed "a period of law study at least substantially equivalent in duration" to the period of law study required of an applicant educated in an "approved law school."[8]

Further, the applicant who studied law in another country must fulfill an additional requirement. Here, the applicant has two alternatives. Under the first alternative, the applicant must show that such country's "jurisprudence is based upon the principles of the English Common Law" and that the applicant's legal education was "the substantial equivalent of the legal education provided by an approved law school in the United States."[9] Alternatively, if the additional requirement cannot

---

[6] Id. § 520.5.

[7] Id. § 520.5(c).

[8] Id. § 520.5(b).

[9] Id. § 520.5(b)(1).

be fulfilled in this way, then the applicant must meet one of two conditions: either the applicant must successfully complete a program of at least 24 semester hours "in professional law subjects in an approved law school in the United States"; or the applicant must meet "the educational requirements for admission to an approved law school in the United States for an LL.M. or S.J.D. degree in law."[10]

Admission to the Bar Without Examination

The New York courts have discretionary authority to admit to the Bar, without examination, an applicant who is over 26 years of age, who has had "the substantial equivalent" of the legal education required for "a first degree in law" from an "approved law school," and who meets certain other conditions. These other conditions can be met by an applicant who has been admitted to practice, and while admitted has actually practiced for a period of at least five of the immediately preceding seven years, either "in the highest law court" in a United States jurisdiction, or "as an attorney- and counselor-at-law or the equivalent in the highest court in another country whose jurisprudence is based upon the principles of the English Common Law."[11]

---

[10] Id. § 520.5(b)(2). These provisions are significantly more liberal for an applicant from a non-English Common Law jurisdiction than the provisions as originally proposed on July 3, 1979. See 417 N.Y.S.2d No. 3 p. 27, pp. 32-34. Such an applicant, however, may not qualify by studying law in the office of a New York attorney. Cf. id. § 520.5(c)(2)(i).

[11] N.Y. Rules §§ 520.9(a)-(d). The proof required is set forth in §§ 520.9(b), (c), and § 520.9(d) gives the courts discretion to impose "other tests of character and fitness." On June 29, 1984 (effective September 1, 1984), the New York Court of Appeals added to § 520.9(a)(2)(i) the requirement that the five-year period of practice be during the immediately preceding seven years.

Legal Consultants

On June 6, 1974, the New York Court of Appeals adopted Rules for Licensing of Legal Consultants, permitting the licensing of applicants who are attorneys (or the equivalent) in foreign countries and have practiced and been in good standing for at least five of the immediately preceding seven years.[12] The applicant must be of good moral character, must reside in the state and must be at least 26 years of age.[13] Section 53(6) of the New York Judiciary Law provides that the licensed legal consultant "shall not practice in the courts of the state but may render legal services in the state within limitations prescribed in rules adopted by the court of appeals."[14] Pursuant to those rules, the legal consultant is authorized to engage in a consulting practice but may not prepare instruments that affect: (1) title to real estate located in the U.S.; (2) disposition on death of property located in and owned by a U.S. resident; (3) administration of a decedent's estate in the U.S.; or (4) marital relations of, or custody of a child of, a U.S. resident.

---

[12] [1983] 22 N.Y.C.R.R. Part 521, § 521.1(a). Effective November 1, 1983, the New York Court of Appeals added a new § 521.6, whereby the Court of Appeals "may in its discretion vary the application of or waive any provision of these rules [Part 521] where strict compliance will cause undue hardship to the applicant." The Court announced that this provision "is intended to permit the Court of Appeals to waive professional qualifications where an applicant's practice of law has been terminated by virtue of the political or religious or racial policies of the nation from which he or she has emigrated."

[13] Id. §§ 521.1(b)-(d).

[14] N.Y. Jud. Law § 53(6) (McKinney 1983).

The legal consultant is authorized to give advice on other aspects of the law of New York or of the United States, provided it is based upon the advice of a person (not a legal consultant) "duly qualified and entitled" to render such advice.[15] Legal consultants in New York are free to practice on their own (under a firm name or individually) or in conjunction with American lawyers. The proper title for a person licensed pursuant to the rules is "legal consultant" or the "authorized title and firm name or either in the foreign country of his admission to practice, in each case in conjunction with the name of such foreign country."[16] A legal consultant may not hold himself out as a member of the New York Bar but is subject to the same disciplinary rules as any member of the New York Bar.[17] As of February 1984, some seventy legal consultants had been licensed pursuant to the applicable rules of the Appellate Division of the Supreme Court of New York.[18]

---

[15] [1983] 22 N.Y.C.R.R. § 521.3.

[16] Id. § 521.3(g).

[17] Id. §§ 521.3(f), 521.4.

[18] [1983] 22 N.Y.C.R.R. Part 610 (1st Dept.), Part 692 (2nd Dept.).

Ohio

The Rules of the Supreme Court of Ohio[1] provide two procedures for admission to the Bar of applicants meeting the general requirements of age (21 years), character and fitness.

First, an applicant (whether or not a citizen of the United States or an Ohio resident) may be admitted by passing the Ohio bar examination if he or she (1) has a degree from a law school which is approved by the American Bar Association and (2) earned prior to admission to law school a bachelor's degree in a college or university approved by the Supreme Court of Ohio or has a record of academic achievement satisfactory to the Supreme Court.[2] An applicant to take the bar examination must submit a certificate from a law school attesting that the applicant has received and successfully completed a course of not less than ten classroom hours of instruction in the Code of Professional Responsibility.[3]

Second, an applicant who is a citizen of the United States and is or intends to become a resident of Ohio may be admitted without passing the bar examination if he or she (1) has been admitted to practice, and is in good standing in the Bar, in another state or the District of Columbia, (2) had at the time of admission in the other state education

---

[1] Supreme Court Rules for the Government of the Bar of Ohio.

[2] Ohio Sup. Ct. Rule I, § 1.

[3] Id. § 4(A)(c).

"equal to" the education required for admission in Ohio by examination and (3) has for at least five years while a nondomiciliary of Ohio engaged in legal work outside Ohio or has for at least five years engaged in the full-time teaching of law at a law school approved by the American Bar Association.[4]

Under both procedures special provision is made for evaluation by the Supreme Court of Ohio of an applicant's undergraduate or legal education that was not received in the United States.[5] A committee of the League of Ohio Law Schools assists the Supreme Court in making that evaluation.[6]

---

4 Id. § 9.

5 Id. §§ 2(A)(g), 9(A)(k).

6 See Turack, "Access to the State Bar Examination for Foreign-Trained Graduates: The Ohio Experience," 8 Ohio N.U.L. Rev. 265, 273-276 (1981).

Pennsylvania

Admission to the Bar of Pennsylvania requires (1) the completion of legal studies at a law school accredited by the ABA; (2) a degree from an accredited college or university, or satisfaction of the Pennsylvania Board of Law Examiners that the equivalent education has been obtained; (3) successful completion of the bar examination; and (4) absence of conduct indicating incompatibility with the Bar's standards of character and general qualifications.[1] Moreover, admission without examination is permitted in the discretion of the State Board if an applicant has been admitted before the highest court of a state granting reciprocity,[2] has submitted a good standing certificate from the highest court of such state together with proof either of engaging in the practice of law in such state or of teaching full-time in an accredited law school for at least five of the seven years preceding the application, and has fulfilled the same moral character and pre-legal education requirements required for applicants taking the bar examination.[3]

A foreign lawyer may be deemed to have obtained an "equivalent education" if he completed the study of law in a law school outside

---

[1] Pa. R. Ct., Bar Admission Rule 203. A residency requirement was eliminated by the Pennsylvania Supreme Court in 1983.

[2] Rule 102 defines "reciprocal state" as a state having a reciprocal agreement or arrangement with the Commonwealth of Pennsylvania concerning admission to the Bar. Pa. R. Ct., Bar Admission Rule 102.

[3] Id. Rule 204.

of the United States and is a member in good standing at the Bar of a foreign country, as evidenced by a certificate of good standing issued by the relevant foreign court or agency.[4] Moreover, in order to apply to sit for the bar examination, a foreign lawyer must have successfully completed a total of 24 credit hours of legal study at an accredited U.S. law school in any of the following subjects, with no more than 4 credit hours in any one subject counting toward this requirement:[5] conflicts of law; constitutional law; contracts; corporations; criminal law; decedent's estates; evidence; family law; federal civil procedure; federal income taxes (personal only); professional responsibility; real property; torts; Uniform Commercial Code, Art. II - Sales; Uniform Commercial Code, Art. III - Commercial Paper; Uniform Commercial Code, Art. IX - Secured Transactions.

The current rule clearly seems intended to facilitate qualifying to sit for the Pennsylvania bar examination in the case of a lawyer educated outside the U.S. There is, however, no provision for admission without examination that would apply to lawyers from foreign countries. The International and Comparative Law Section of the Pennsylvania Bar Association has for several years urged adoption of rules similar to the legal consultant rules adopted in New York. A difference between the Pennsylvania proposal and the New York rules is that the former would

---

[4] Id. Rule 205.

[5] Id.

not require a showing of "actual residence" in the Commonwealth, but instead would require that the applicant's principal place of business be Pennsylvania during the time the license was in effect. In addition, the Pennsylvania license would be effective for a period of not more than three years, and would be renewable within six months of its expiration. As of January 1984, the Section's recommendation had not been acted on.

Texas

Generally, admission to the organized legal profession of Texas requires successful completion of the bar examination. In order to be eligible for the examination, an applicant must (1) possess the required "educational attainments" (see below), (2) be a resident of Texas either on the examination date or at the time of licensing, (3) be either a citizen of the United States or lawfully admitted to the United States for permanent residence,[1] and (4) be at least 18 years old and of good moral character and fitness.[2] Although there are a few statutory exemptions from the bar examination requirement, the applicability of such statutory exemptions to attorneys from jurisdictions outside the United States is unclear.[3]

In addition to the other requirements of eligibility to take the bar examination, the rules adopted by the Supreme Court of Texas pro-

---

1 No reported cases have decided the issue of whether, following the decision of the U.S. Supreme Court in In re Griffiths, 413 U.S. 717 (1973), a state may deny admission to the Bar on grounds that a non-citizen who is lawfully residing in the United States is not a "permanent resident" under the immigration laws.

2 Tex. R. Ct., Rules Governing Admission to the Bar of Texas, Rule II.

3 The exemptions include one for a "foreign" attorney "if the applicant has practiced law for three years and has a license to practice law issued by another state or territory or by the District of Columbia, and the licensing standards of the state or territory or the District of Columbia are equivalent to or exceed those of this state"; this exemption is apparently limited to attorneys licensed within U.S. jurisdictions. See Tex. Rev. Civ. Stat. Ann. Article 308(a) (Vernon Supp. 1982).

vide a detailed procedure for filing a Declaration of Intention to Study Law within 120 days after beginning law studies.[4] If an applicant does not make timely filing of a Declaration, a "reasonable excuse" may be submitted to the Board of Examiners in writing, which may result in delayed admission to the examination until the Declaration has been on file for at least 270 days.[5] Presumably, a non-U.S. citizen's absence from the jurisdiction would constitute a "reasonable excuse" within the meaning of this rule.

Legal education requirements can be fulfilled by graduation from an "approved law school," i.e., one officially approved by the American Bar Association.[6]

Although it is unclear whether the statutory exemptions to the bar examination requirements apply to attorneys licensed in jurisdictions outside the United States, the Supreme Court rules provide some relief from the eligibility requirements to take the bar examination for "[a]ny licensed attorney at law immigrating or who has heretofore immigrated to this state from a foreign country."[7] Such an applicant must (1) be either a citizen of the United States or an alien lawfully admitted to the

---

[4] Tex. R. Ct., Rules Governing Admission to the Bar of Texas, Rule III.

[5] Id. Rule III(c).

[6] Id. Rule IV.

[7] Id. Rule VIII(b).

United States for permanent residence,[8] (2) show that for at least seven years he or she has been duly licensed to practice law in the highest court of the nation of his or her former residence, (3) show that for at least seven of the ten years immediately preceding the filing of the application he or she has been lawfully engaged in the practice of law as his or her principal means of livelihood, (4) never have been disbarred or had his or her license suspended or had misconduct charges pending against him or her, (5) furnish to the Board of Law Examiners evidence as to his or her moral character and fitness, and (6) show, to the satisfaction of the Board of Law Examiners,

> that the applicant has graduated from a law school which requires legal study for a comparable length of time as is required by approved law schools for graduation, that the licensing standards in the nation in which the applicant has a license to practice are equivalent to or exceed the licensing requirements of this State, except the requirement of graduation from an approved law school, and that the law of said nation is basically common law and is sufficiently comparable to the law of this State as in the judgment of the Board [of Law Examiners] will enable the applicant to become a competent attorney in this State without additional formal legal education.[9]

After meeting these requirements, the applicant may be admitted to the examination and, upon passing the examination, may be issued a temporary certificate to practice law in Texas for a period of one year from the date of its issuance unless it is sooner revoked or cancelled by the Board of Law Examiners[10]. The rules further state that:

---

[8] *See* note 1, *supra*.

[9] *Id.* Rule VIII(b)(1), (2).

[10] *Id.* Rule VIII(b)(3).

> Provided the said temporary certificate is still in good standing at the expiration of one year from the date of its issuance, an applicant who has continuously resided and practiced law in Texas during such one year period may upon recommendation of the Board be granted a license to practice law in this State. The applicant shall make written request to the Board for a license no more than sixty days nor less than thirty days prior to the expiration of the temporary certificate. The Board may, before making such a recommendation, adopt any means within its discretion for the purpose of satisfying itself that the applicant while practicing law during such period has demonstrated that the applicant possesses the character, qualifications, and fitness to receive a license to practice law in this State.[11]

Thus, the admission to the Texas Bar of an attorney licensed in a foreign jurisdiction rests, to a large extent, in the discretion of the Board of Law Examiners and greatly depends upon the facts surrounding the individual application.

---

[11] Id. Rule VIII(a)(6).

II. Regulation of American Lawyers in Sixteen Foreign Jurisdictions; European Community.

Summary

The sixteen foreign jurisdictions reviewed below are Australia, Belgium, Brazil, Canada, China, England, France, West Germany, Hong Kong, Israel, Italy, Japan, Mexico, The Netherlands, Nigeria and Singapore. Belgium, England, France, West Germany, Italy and The Netherlands are within the European Community and therefore are subject to the Community's rules governing lawyers who are nationals of the Community's Member States. These rules are described at page 105 below under the caption "Rules of the European Community".

Analysis by Foreign Jurisdiction

Australia

Each of the six states and two territories of Australia[1] has separate legislation covering the recognition of qualifications in law, and some differences exist in their requirements. At present, admission to practice in one state or territory does not necessarily entitle a practitioner to practice in another state or territory.

The profession is represented and controlled by professional bodies which together have established the Law Council of Australia to represent the profession on a national basis. However, the acceptance and recognition of professional qualifications, both academic and practical, and admission to practice are the responsibility of the courts or of registration boards established by statute.

Practitioners usually decide early in their careers to function as either solicitors or barristers, although to some extent the practice varies between different states and territories. In New South Wales and Queensland the two branches of the profession are separated. Victoria admits lawyers as barristers and solicitors, but in practice separation does exist and on admission those who wish to do so sign the roll of barristers. In all other states and territories both branches of the profes-

---

[1] New South Wales, Victoria, Western Australia, Queensland, Tasmania, South Australia, the Australian Capital Territory and the Northern Territory.

sion are fused; nevertheless, in each of them a separate grouping of those choosing to practice as barristers has been formed. Although, ordinarily, the functions of advocate are performed by the barristers, solicitors have right of audience in all courts, both state and federal.

There are some 20,000 practicing lawyers in Australia. In New South Wales (the capital of which is Sydney) there are 950 barristers and 7,700 solicitors and in Victoria (capital Melbourne) 860 barristers and 5,070 solicitors.

Generally speaking, to satisfy the necessary educational requirements an approved degree from an Australian university is required. In addition there is usually a requirement of a period of practical experience in a solicitor's office or, alternatively, satisfactory completion of an approved course in practical legal education.

When considering applications for admission to practice from lawyers qualified outside Australia, the various admitting authorities take into account the periods during which applicants have practiced in their own countries. At their discretion the authorities may choose to exempt foreign applicants from parts of the qualifying examinations. Generally speaking, practitioners from the United Kingdom and New Zealand are admitted to practice, and to varying degrees the qualifications obtained in other British Commonwealth countries are recognized.

No general rule can be stated as to whether United States lawyers can obtain any exemption in respect of their American qualifications, and this question can only be answered in particular cases when applicants submit their American qualifications, together with details of their experience, to the admitting authority in the relevant Australian state or territory. It is usual for examination in certain subjects to be required and for a period of practical training to be imposed.

Two examples of reciprocal admission arrangements may be taken. At one end of the scale is the Victorian position, which until the present time has been the state chosen by many overseas practitioners for entry into Australia. There is no need in Victoria to show three years post-admission experience in the foreign country (a requirement in some other Australian jurisdictions) and, because there are no residency requirements, the admission process is simplified. Victorian admission provides a useful prerequisite to admission in other Australian jurisdictions. However, changes to the Victorian requirements have made admission more difficult and further changes are in prospect in both Victoria and other jurisdictions. Accordingly, it cannot be assumed that the "Victorian springboard" will continue to be available for admission in other states.

At the other end of the scale, Queensland is the main exception to the general rule that there is reciprocity of admission between the various states and territories. For admission in Queensland a solicitor must establish that he intends at the time of his admission to be in bona fide practice or employment in Queensland for at least nine months of the year immediately succeeding such admission. Furthermore, Queensland restrictions on the use of firm names and on fee-sharing with practitioners outside the state effectively limit the extent to which an interstate firm can practice in Queensland under its own name.

The present arrangements may not continue indefinitely, as a committee under the chairmanship of the Chief Justice of New South Wales is engaged in the task of reform of the interstate and overseas admission rules. The tentative direction of reform[2] includes the following:

1. All law degrees (whether obtained in Australia or elsewhere) will be tested against a common core of legal subjects. The content of this core has not been finally determined. Recent developments in Victoria suggest that there will be pressure to adopt a core of 12 subjects as the norm throughout Australia. This follows from the recommendations of the unpublished McGarvie Report wherein the Victorian Council of Legal Education advised (on October 14, 1982) that the following 12 subjects should compose the new Victorian core, viz: legal process, criminal law and procedure, torts, contracts, property, trusts, administrative law, Federal and State constitutional law, civil procedure, evidence, professional conduct and accounting.
2. Interstate admissions should be treated on a uniform basis with full and immediate reciprocity.

---

[2] The direction of reform is discussed generally in Walker, "Reforming Inter-State and Overseas Admission Rules in Australia: A Strategy for New Zealand," New Zealand L.J. (June 1983).

See also proposed statutory rules 10, 11 and 12 of the Victorian Council of Legal Education.

3. The status of persons already admitted to practice overseas will be completely reviewed. It seems unlikely that a privileged status will continue to be granted to United Kingdom admissions.

Australian or British citizenship is no longer necessary for admission in most Australian jurisdictions, and the requirement for an oath of allegiance can be waived, for example, in the case of American citizens.

There may be difficulties in several states and territories (including Queensland) for a foreign firm to establish an office in its own name. In these jurisdictions, only a name may be used which represents the names of present or previous partners. It is believed that at the present time there are only two foreign firms practicing under their own names, one of which has offices in Sydney and Melbourne and the other in Melbourne. In each case the resident partners are locally qualified.

Foreign lawyers will also be required to investigate current immigration policy in Australia, as it is now difficult for a foreign lawyer to obtain permanent resident status in Australia. Most successful applications for a visa are now based on grounds such as existing family relationships in Australia. The alternative basis of an employer's nomination requires evidence that the applicant's skills are not available locally.

Belgium

The practice of law in Belgium is divided into three professions: (1) avocats, to whom practice before the Belgian courts is reserved by law; (2) notaires, semi-public officials with exclusive authority to effect certain transactions (such as the creation of bodies corporate and the transfer of real property); and (3) conseillers juridiques, legal counselors who are entitled to give legal advice. An avocat must be a member of one of the Belgian Bars; the notaires have their own, separate professional organization; a Belgian legal education is a prerequisite for membership in either profession. The profession of the conseillers juridiques, on the other hand, is not formally organized or subject to legal regulation and may be practiced by all Belgians as well as by non-Belgians who have been authorized to reside and work in Belgium.

In order to reside and work in Belgium, a lawyer who is a national of a non-Common Market country must obtain a visa and either a work permit or a professional card. For such a lawyer who meets the legal definition of an "employee," a work permit is appropriate and must be requested and obtained by the employer. Such a lawyer who is a resident partner of a law firm, on the other hand, or who seeks independently to engage in professional activity in Belgium, must obtain a professional card.

While the professional card may contain restrictions on the lawyer's permitted activities in Belgium, the Belgian Government and the U.S. Embassy in Brussels have sought to avoid the imposition of unreasonable restrictions. The right of American lawyers to engage in legal counseling in Belgium is supported by the 1961 Treaty of Friendship, Establishment and Navigation between Belgium and the United States, which provides that nationals of each country may establish offices in the other country upon conditions no less favorable than those accorded the nationals of such other country.[1]

In 1984, the Bar Council of Brussels added to its rules new provisions which permit members of non-Belgian Bars to associate with avocats in Brussels.[2] These new rules of the Brussels Bar do not alter the governmental regulations discussed in the two preceeding paragraphs; that is, the new rules do not alter the governmental regulations applicable to non-Common Market lawyers who establish their own offices in Belgium. Under the new rules, Brussels avocats are authorized (1) to form associations in Brussels with members of non-Belgian Bars who register with the Brussels Bar, and (2) to treat members of non-Belgian Bars as associates or, if the foreign lawyers have been registered with the Brussels Bar for at least three years, as partners. Non-Belgian lawyers who practice in Belgium pursuant to the new rules are subject to discipline by, and to the rules of, the Brussels Bar. The forms of association which will be permitted under these new rules are as yet (July 1984) unclear.

---

1 [1961] 14 U.S.T. 1284, T.I.A.S. No. 5432.

2 Reglement d'Ordre Interieur de l'Ordre des Avocats du Barreau de Bruxelles, arts. 69-79 (1984).

Brazil

The Charter of the Brazilian Bar Association contains provisions relating to the admission of Brazilians and foreigners to the Brazilian Bar. Requirements for admission include: (1) civil capacity; (2) a bachelor of laws degree, or its equivalent, "formalized as provided by law"; (3) submission of evidence that the applicant has satisfied a clerkship requirement or has passed the bar examination; and (4) general requirements as to character and fitness to practice law.[1] For foreigners, there is a further requirement of reciprocity for Brazilians in the applicant's country of origin. U.S. attorneys must prove that Brazilians could be admitted in the jurisdiction of their admission in the United States.

In the case of a lawyer (Brazilian or foreign) who is a graduate of a foreign law school rather than a Brazilian law school, the foreign law degree must be recognized by a Brazilian law school as equivalent to the degree which that law school confers. Resolution No. 43 of the Federal Council of Education provides that the equivalency determination must be made through a process of "revalidation" of the applicant's diploma and registration with the Ministry of Education and Culture.[2]

Only an accredited Brazilian university (rather than an independent law faculty) may revalidate a foreign law diploma. No univer-

---

[1] Charter of the Brazilian Bar Association (Ordem dos Advogados do Brasil), Law No. 4.215 (April 27, 1963), Article 48 (hereinafter, the "OAB Charter").

[2] Resolution No. 43 of the Federal Council of Education [Brazil] (December 18, 1975).

sity, however, is obligated to revalidate a foreign diploma, and a candidate may find that a number of universities will decline to undertake the revalidation process.

The process consists of proving the course of study, and the authenticity of the foreign diploma, to the office of the rector of the university. The candidate must also prove that he was graduated from an accredited secondary school and submit copies of all his transcripts notarized, legalized in a Brazilian Consulate and translated. Once satisfied on these points, the office of the rector customarily remits the proceeding to the law faculty of the university with instructions to review the course of study, to determine the procedures that are necessary to complement the foreign course of study in such a manner that it will be equivalent to the requirement for the equivalent degree in Brazil from that university, and to administer those procedures.

The law faculty of the chosen university customarily administers examinations in most of the subjects taught at the law school. The range of subjects on which the candidate may be examined includes civil law, civil procedure, commercial law, administrative law, public finance, private international law, criminal law, criminal procedure, constitutional law and labor law. There are no rules regarding what is sufficient to complement the foreign course of study, and each law faculty has ample discretion to determine what it considers necessary to have the candidate qualify for a degree from the institution.

Once satisfied that the candidate has successfully demonstrated equivalency, the law faculty remits the proceeding to the office of the rector, who, in turn, annotates the revalidation on the diploma. The diploma is then registered at the university and at the Ministry of Education and Culture.

A valid Brazilian law diploma is but one of the requirements for admission to the Brazilian Bar. A foreign lawyer seeking admission must also either successfully pass a bar examination or complete a clerkship. Because a clerkship ("estágio") is in effect available only to students in the fourth and fifth years of law school, a foreign lawyer who revalidates his diploma must take the bar examination.[3]

The bar examination is given four times a year and is administered locally by each regional section. It consists of both a written and an oral examination. A failure to obtain a grade of 3 (on a scale of 0 to 10) on the written examination precludes taking the oral examination and constitutes failure. To pass, the candidate must obtain a minimum average grade of 5 on the written and oral examinations.[4]

---

[3] It is possible that a foreign lawyer graduated from law school during or prior to 1973 may be exempted from the bar examination. See Law No. 5.960 of December 10, 1973, which exempts persons from taking the bar examination if they were graduated from law school in 1973 or before. In a recent case in Rio de Janeiro, the regional section exempted one foreign lawyer from the bar examination on this ground. In a subsequent case with the same facts, however, the same body held (in a split decision) that "graduation from law school" meant Brazilian revalidation of the diploma, and the candidate was required to take the bar examination.

[4] See Provision No. 34 of the Federal Council of the Brazilian Bar Association (Oct. 4, 1967).

The bar examination covers civil law and procedure, criminal law and procedure, labor law and procedure, professional ethics and judicial organization. In Rio de Janeiro and São Paulo, the percentage of those who pass the bar examination is reported to be often less than 50%.

Although the "practice of law" is broadly defined in Brazilian law to include everything from representation of clients in courts and administrative proceedings to legal work of a consulting or advisory nature,[5] the activities exclusive to lawyers are basically those relating to litigation.[6] Any acts exclusive to lawyers which are carried out by persons not registered in the Brazilian Bar Association are null and void.[7] In addition, any person not registered in the Brazilian Bar Association who holds himself out as a lawyer is subject to criminal sanctions.[8]

There are currently no special procedures for licensing foreign lawyers to practice in the capacity of legal consultants.

---

5 See OAB Charter, Article 71.

6 Id., Article 71, § 3.

7 Id., Article 76.

8 Id., Article 128; Decree-Law No. 3.688, Article 47 (October 3, 1941).

Canada

Each of the ten provinces[1] and two territories[2] of Canada has its own requirements for admission to the practice of law. While the legal profession is separately organized and governed in each of these jurisdictions, they have in common the Canadian Bar Association and the Federation of Law Societies of Canada. In addition, to provide advice on the accreditation of lawyers educated outside Canada, the Federation has established a Joint Committee on Foreign Accreditation.[3] The rulings of this Committee are accepted for purposes of accreditation in some but not all instances.

The rules and procedures of the various provinces often allow a lawyer to receive Canadian recognition of academic qualifications obtained in the United States. Notwithstanding this possibility, however, to be licensed to practice in Canada a lawyer usually must be a Canadian citizen (or, alternatively, in some provinces, a British subject). A requirement of this nature in Ontario was recently challenged on the grounds that it violated provisions of the recently-enacted Canadian Charter of Rights and Freedoms[4] guaranteeing freedom of mobility within Canada to Cana-

---

[1] Alberta, British Columbia, Manitoba, New Brunswick, Newfoundland, Nova Scotia, Ontario, Prince Edward Island, Quebec, Saskatchewan.

[2] Northwest Territories, Yukon Territory.

[3] Located at the Faculty of Law, University of Ottawa, Ottawa, Ontario K1N 6N5.

[4] Constitution Act of 1981, Schedule B.

dian citizens and landed immigrants. In Law Society of Upper Canada v. Skapinker,[5] the Supreme Court of Canada held that the citizenship requirement did not violate the mobility provisions of the Charter, but did not rule on its constitutionality with respect to the other provisions of the Charter.

Each province has educational requirements for admission to practice and, depending upon the province, there may be additional requirements, such as a mandatory bar admission course, an examination in specified subjects, and a period of clerkship.

Although the requirement that a licensed lawyer must be a Canadian citizen (or a British subject) operates effectively to exclude United States citizens from the permanent practice of law in Canada, some flexibility exists in three provinces with respect to United States citizens who have declared their intention to become Canadian citizens.

In Newfoundland, a person who is not a Canadian citizen can be admitted to practice if such person is a landed immigrant in Canada and, in the judgment of the Law Society of Newfoundland, cannot become a Canadian citizen for reasons beyond his control or for other good reasons.[6] In order to be admitted, a person must have a Canadian law de-

---

[5] Law Society of Upper Canada v. Skapinker, File No. 17537 (May 3, 1984).

[6] The Law Society Act, Nfld. Rev. Stat. ch. 77, § 39(3) (June 17, 1977).

gree or its foreign equivalent (as determined by the Education Committee of the Law Society).[7]

In Manitoba, a United States citizen, otherwise qualified, can be admitted to practice if "he has been lawfully admitted to Canada for permanent residence";[8] however, "if he fails to become a Canadian citizen within a period of four years after he has been lawfully admitted to Canada for permanent residence he shall cease to be entitled to carry on the practice or profession of barrister or solicitor in Manitoba."[9]

In New Brunswick, a United States citizen who meets certain requirements can qualify for admission as a barrister and solicitor if the applicant has been admitted to Canada for permanent residence and declares "that he has applied or intends, as soon as he is eligible, to apply for Canadian citizenship."[10] But such a lawyer will be disbarred in New Brunswick if "within six years of filing the declaration" he does not become a Canadian citizen.[11] The New Brunswick applicant who is a United States citizen must have been engaged in active practice for at least three of the five years immediately preceding the application, must pass exami-

---

7 Id. § 38.

8 The Law Society Act, Man. Rev. Stat. ch. L-100, § 36(1).

9 Id. § 36(2).

10 Barristers' Society Act, N.B. Rev. Stat. ch. 80, § 9(3), as amended; Regulations of the Barristers' Society of New Brunswick § 32(1).

11 Barristers' Society Act, N.B. Rev Stat. ch. 80, § 13(3).

nations on the Canadian Constitution and designated Canadian statutes, and must be in good standing "in the last jurisdiction in which he practiced prior to his application."[12]

Various provinces have provisions for the admission to practice, on an occasional or regular basis, of lawyers who have been admitted in other provinces. The extent, if any, to which a United States citizen admitted in one province could invoke such a provision in another province is, however, unclear. In certain provinces, such as Prince Edward Island, Nova Scotia, Alberta, Ontario and Saskatchewan, it seems unlikely that a United States citizen could be admitted to practice on a regular basis even if the citizen had been admitted to the Bar in another province.[13] In Alberta, an applicant can serve under articles while awaiting citizenship but must be a Canadian citizen to be admitted to practice. In Ontario, an applicant for admission to practice law may serve under articles and may attend courses preparatory for admission to the Bar but may not be actually admitted before becoming a Canadian citizen (or British subject). In Saskatchewan, a Canadian citizen (or British subject) who has been admitted to practice in the United States may be admitted to

---

[12] Regulations of the Barristers' Society of New Brunswick § 32(2).

[13] _See_ The Law Society and Legal Professions Act as amended, P.E.I. Rev. Stat. cap. L-9, § 15(a); Regulations of the Nova Scotia Barristers' Society § 16(a); The Legal Profession Act, Alta. Rev. Stat. ch. L-9, §§ 39,40; The Law Society Act, Ont. Rev. Stat. ch. 233, § 28 (1980); The Legal Profession Act, Sask. Rev. Stat. ch. L-10, § 35(2).

practice under certain circumstances without further study if he can pass certain examinations and serves under articles for one year. In Quebec, an occasional appearance rule applies more generally to advocates from any of the other provinces in Canada.

By and large, Canadian provincial legislation defines the practice of law in broad terms, encompassing all matters before the courts and all legal counseling, and does not authorize persons to carry on such a practice unless they have been licensed to do so.[14] In most instances, practitioners are referred to either as "barristers and solicitors" or as "barristers or solicitors" and, in practice (if not in terminology), they are members of a single, fused legal profession.[15] In Quebec, there is a Bar (Barreau) consisting of practicing advocates (avocats) who must be Canadian citizens,[16] and solicitors (conseillers en loi) who are either (1) members of the Bar of another province who practice in an organization that has its head office or its subsidiary in the province of Quebec and who undertake to act within the limits of the functions authorized by the Bar Act for the exclusive account of their employer or its subsidiaries,[17]

---

[14] See, e.g., Province of New Brunswick, Barristers' Society Act ch. 80, §§ 14, 15; The Law Society Act, Man. Rev. Stat. ch. L-100, § 48; Quebec, Bar Act, 15-16 Eliz. II, c. 77, §§ 128-43; The Legal Profession Act, Sask. Rev. Stat. ch. L-10, § 5.

[15] The Regulations of the Nova Scotia Barristers' Society § 15(1)(b) are exceptionally limpid in dealing with the terminology problem and define "barrister" to include "solicitor."

[16] Quebec, Bar Act, 15-16 Eliz. II, c. 77, § 45.

[17] Id. § 62.

or (2) non-Canadian citizens who are professors who have been teaching for at least three years in a law faculty or a department of legal studies which grants a degree recognized by the provincial government.[18] Finally, a separate legal profession of notaries (notaires) exists in Quebec with broad privileges; their "chief duty is to draw up and execute deeds and contracts" when the parties desire notarial authenticity.[19] Only Canadian citizens can become notaries.[20]

---

[18] Id. § 62(a).

[19] Notarial Act, S.Q. 1968 c. 70, as amended, § 2.

[20] Id. § 120(b).

China

Provisional regulations for lawyers of the People's Republic of China came into effect on January 1, 1982, following three decades without formal rules for lawyers (lushi). The new regulations define lawyers as "workers of the state" and set forth the specific qualifications, duties and rights of lawyers in China, as well as the organizational structure within which lawyers shall work. Under this definition, there are currently 6,000 lawyers in China, although the Chinese government hopes to train an additional 29,000 lawyers before the year 2000.

Admission to practice as a lawyer is limited to citizens of the People's Republic of China who support the socialist system, who have the right to elect and be elected, and who fit at least one of the following descriptions: (1) graduates from law colleges who have more than two years' experience in judicial work, teaching of law or research on legal affairs; (2) persons with legal training who have worked as judges in people's courts or as people's procurators; (3) persons who have completed university education and worked in the areas of economics, science or technology for more than three years, who have knowledge of laws and statutes relevant to their work and who have received legal training; or (4) persons who have legal knowledge and experience equivalent to those specified in (1) or (2) above and who have acquired an educational level equivalent to university students and are suitable to practice as lawyers.

Persons who meet qualifications (1) or (2) above may be issued licenses to practice law after a two-year period of probation which commences following examination and approval by the judiciary department of the province, autonomous region or municipality where the individual will practice. All persons who practice as lawyers may be licensed only following examinations by the judiciary department (bureau) of the province, autonomous region or municipality, and should be reported to the Ministry of Justice of the People's Republic of China for the record.

Persons who are qualified to practice law but are unable to leave their professional work may be engaged as part-time lawyers, except that persons holding posts in a people's court, people's procuratorate or people's public security organ are prohibited from working as part-time lawyers.

Qualified lawyers may be assigned to give legal advice to individual citizens as well as government agencies, enterprises, institutions and public organizations in either litigious or non-litigious cases and matters. In addition, lawyers may be entrusted by litigants in civil cases to act as their attorneys, may be entrusted or appointed to act as advocates for plaintiffs or defendants in criminal cases, may act as attorneys in mediation or arbitration, and may draft pleadings and other legal documents.

Lawyers are entitled to perform their duties only under the auspices of legal counsel offices, which are defined as "institutions under the leadership and supervision of the judicial administrative organs of the state." At the present time, legal counsel offices are being set up in counties, cities and municipal districts. Specialized legal counsel offices may be set up, if necessary, on the approval of the Ministry of Justice. The legal counsel offices are to receive commissions and collect fees on behalf of the lawyers.

While there are no provisions which permit foreign lawyers to practice in China, the employment of foreign legal consultants (including American lawyers) by state organizations and enterprises has been allowed. Foreign lawyers have also been permitted to act on behalf of foreign clients in mediation and arbitration, although they cannot legally appear in Chinese courts on behalf of clients. There also are no provisions regarding the establishment of a foreign law office or branch office in China, and to date no foreign law firm has been permitted to register an office in China. The subject of foreign lawyers is a relatively new issue in China, having come under review by the Ministry of Justice and other specialized groups in recent years. It is possible that further clarification regarding the regulation of foreign lawyers in China will be made in the future.

England

The legal profession in England (including Wales) is at the time of writing (April 1984) in a state of flux. The present position is stated first and then a brief indication given of changes possible in the next few years.

Present Position

The profession is divided into two branches, namely solicitors and barristers. There are some 37,000 solicitors in private practice and about 5,000 barristers. The main function of the solicitors is to give general and, where appropriate, specialist advice, to conduct the day-to-day legal business of the client, to appear as advocates in the lower courts and before administrative tribunals, and to prepare many of the papers for trials in superior courts in which barristers will be undertaking the advocacy. Barristers, who have the exclusive right of audience before the superior courts, largely concentrate on advocacy and pre-trial preparatory work, although some barristers develop extensive advisory practices, particularly in specialist fields. While solicitors normally practice in partnership, barristers may not practice in partnership (though they normally share premises known as "chambers"). In general, by reason of the Bar's own Practice Rules, the lay client cannot instruct a barrister except through a solicitor, the legal work in the case being divided between the two on a conventionally agreed basis.

British citizenship is not required to become a barrister or solicitor. Admission to the profession is controlled in the case of barristers by the Senate of the Inns of Court and the Bar, and in the case of solicitors by The Law Society. The Bar generally requires of entrants at least a second-class honors university degree (not necessarily in law). While a university degree is not obligatory for solicitors, some 90% of newly admitted solicitors normally have a degree. Both branches require university or other prescribed academic study of the law, comprehensive legal examinations, and practical training in a clerkship with a practicing member of the profession - one year for barristers and at least two for solicitors. Certain relaxations are available as to education, examination and clerkship requirements, depending upon an applicant's previous legal experience and qualifications.[1]

Use of the title "barrister" or "solicitor" and a limited number of "reserved activities" - principally, rights of audience before the courts, the preparation of certain documents (namely those transferring land), and the undertaking of probate work - are reserved to qualified barristers or solicitors.[2] Otherwise, the practice of law in England is not restricted to qualified English lawyers, nor is there any statutory or other system for licensing foreign lawyers to practice in England. In consequence, an American lawyer who has obtained the relevant immigration consent or employment permit to take up residence in England as a

---

[1] For solicitors, see Solicitors Act 1974 §§ 1-5; The Law Society Qualifying Regulations 1979 (as amended).

[2] For solicitors, see Solicitors Act 1974 §§ 20-23.

self-employed or employed practitioner is free to practice the law of the United States or any other jurisdiction, including England, subject only to the above-mentioned matters which are reserved to the English profession.

With regard to immigration controls, an American law firm that wishes to establish an office in England must, for each partner to be based in England (or, if there is to be no such partner, for the associate-in-charge), make application well in advance to the Secretary of State for Home Affairs ("Home Office") for a Letter of Consent which the lawyer can produce to the immigration officer at the port of entry when first arriving in England to take up residence. Subsequent partners must at least in theory go through the same procedure but, once the branch office is established, associates coming from the United States should instead be covered by an Employment Permit obtained from the Department of Employment by the branch office itself. In practice it is believed that in some instances subsequent partners joining established branch offices have availed themselves of the more expeditious Employment Permit procedure.

The application to the Home Office will normally be referred to The Law Society to ascertain whether it has any objections. In order to respond, the Society requires evidence of the applicant's professional qualifications, a certificate of admission and fitness to practice (or similar official letter of commendation or good standing), a brief curriculum vitae, with some details of the applicant's firm, and the names of three or four British references at least one of whom should be an English barrister or solicitor. It is also the Home Office practice to require a short (one page) Undertaking, whereby the applicant undertakes that, if granted permission to reside in the United Kingdom for the purpose of practicing as a consultant in American law, he (a) will not attempt to act or in any way represent himself as qualified to act as an English barrister or solicitor, (b) will observe the standards of conduct of the solicitors branch of the legal profession in England, (c) will not advertise or announce any specialist qualifications on his stationery, and (d) will not share fees with persons not legally qualified.

Neither the Letter of Consent nor the subsequent entry permit endorsed on the passport at the time of entry expresses any limitations on what the American firm and its lawyers may do. An American lawyer established in England, like other individuals who have not qualified as English barristers or solicitors, may not, of course, undertake the reserved activities mentioned above. However, a foreign lawyer, whether established in England or not, may instruct a barrister direct (without the intermediary of a solicitor) in a wide variety of matters not involving United Kingdom litigation.[3]

American lawyers established in England may also apply to The Law Society for the grant of "Overseas Lawyer" status.[4] Although such status does not alter the legal position set out above, nor entitle the law-

---

3 Bye-laws of The Law Society § 14A

4 The Overseas Practice Rules of the Bar (as amended in 1981).

yer to describe himself as a Member of the Society, in effect it confers "club" membership entitling the lawyer to certain privileges, principally use of the library, catering and other facilities at the Society's Hall in London, attendance at the Society's annual conference and eligibility to join certain specialist groups formed within the Society.

Possible Changes

After a relatively quiet period following the Report of the Royal Commission on Legal Services in 1979, strong pressures for change became manifest during 1983 and 1984. These pressures came from within as well as from outside the profession. The principal thrust of these pressures has been to remove from the activities exclusively reserved to the profession the preparation of documents transferring land. The object is to reduce the cost of transfering ownership of residential property.

A Conveyancing Committee has been set up by the Government to examine urgently conditions which might be appropriate for licensing conveyancers, not being barristers or solicitors, to carry out house transfer work for buyers and sellers. The Government also appears committed to allowing banks and building societies (savings and loan associations) to carry out this work using employed solicitors, a proposal which the solicitors profession is contesting.

Moves are also afoot to permit solicitors to advertise their services subject to various suggested restraints, or to none, and possibly to

go into partnership with other professions and services, more particularly accountants, surveyors and estate agents.

The solicitors in turn are seeking rights of audience in the higher courts previously reserved to the Bar and it seems likely that if their request prevails the Bar will change its own rules of professional conduct to permit barristers to accept instructions direct rather than through solicitors, at any rate in non-litigious matters.

The potential implications of these moves for American law firms in England are significant.

France

A law enacted on December 31, 1971 provides for three categories of lawyers in France: (1) the avocat, who has a monopoly of practice before the most important courts, who is authorized to give legal advice and who is governed by an independent Bar; (2) the notaire, who has a monopoly of conveyancing, estate work and the execution of certain formal instruments, and who is governed in part by an independent professional association and in part by the Ministry of Justice; and (3) the conseil juridique (legal counselor), who is authorized to give legal advice and to prepare legal instruments, who is governed by the Ministry of Justice in consultation with an elected body of conseils juridiques, but who is not accorded a monopoly of any aspect of the practice of law. There is also a fourth category of legal professionals which includes miscellaneous advisors who do not fall within the other three categories but who are entitled to give legal advice and prepare legal instruments in the context of their roles as house counsel, real estate agents or labor union or trade association lawyers, or by virtue of being members of the legal professions in other countries of the European Community (EC).[1]

---

[1] The principal statutory and regulatory provisions referred to in this section are found in: Loi No. 71-1130 du 31 décembre 1971 portant réforme de certaines professions judiciaires et juridiques, [1972] J.O. 131 (5 janvier), esp. Titre II, ch. I; and Décret No. 72-670 du 13 juillet 1972 relatif à l'usage du titre de conseil juridique, [1972] J.O. (18 juillet), esp. Titre IV, ch. I, § 3. See generally Professions Judiciaires et Juridiques-Réforme, Brochure No. 1388, Journal Officiel (Paris 1983).

Admission to practice as an <u>avocat</u> or <u>notaire</u> is limited to nationals of EC countries. However, a number of lawyers and law firms from both EC and non-EC countries engage in practice as <u>conseils juridiques</u>.

Registration in the profession of <u>conseil juridique</u> by a foreign lawyer requires graduation from a "recognized" law school and practice for three years of which eighteen months have been practice in France with a qualified <u>conseil juridique</u>. Ordinarily, a diploma from a law school accredited in the U.S. will be recognized in France as equivalent to a French law school diploma. Investigation of the applicant's general character and background is also customary.

Registration in the profession of <u>conseil juridique</u> is required for all individual foreign lawyers who commenced practice in France after July 1, 1971 and who are neither from another EC Member State nor from a nation which accords reciprocal treatment to French lawyers; and their activities are limited to a legal counseling practice involving principally foreign and international law. ("Reciprocal treatment" generally means that a French lawyer in the particular country could conduct the practice there that a French <u>conseil juridique</u> is authorized to conduct in France; the French Government has not indicated that <u>In re Griffiths</u>, combined with New York's rules for licensing legal consultants, constitutes reciprocal U.S. treatment of French lawyers.) Foreign lawyers who commenced practice in France before July 1, 1971, and foreign lawyers from another EC Member State, or a nation which accords reciprocal treatment to

French lawyers, are entitled to register as <u>conseils juridiques</u>, if they desire, and are not bound by the limitation of practice described above.

Foreign law firms which commenced practice in France before July 1, 1971 are also entitled to register as <u>conseils juridiques</u>; and such registration is required for all such law firms which are neither from another EC Member State nor from a nation which accords reciprocal treatment to French lawyers. However, for a foreign firm to register as a <u>conseil juridique</u>, all of its members in France must qualify as <u>conseils juridiques</u>. A foreign law firm which commenced practice in France after July 1, 1971 cannot qualify as a <u>conseil juridique</u>.

The French Government has discretionary authority to limit the activities of registered foreign firms, if they are neither from other EC Member States nor from nations according reciprocal treatment to French lawyers, to a legal counseling practice involving principally foreign and international law. The Government has not indicated an intention to make use of its discretionary authority to limit American law firms in France in this manner.

To practice without registration as a French <u>counseil juridique</u>, an individual foreign lawyer must have been practicing in France prior to July 1, 1971, or must be a national of one of the other EC Member States or of a nation that accords reciprocal treatment to French lawyers.

For a foreign law firm to practice without registration as a French <u>conseil juridique</u>, it must be from either another EC Member State or a nation that accords reciprocal treatment to French lawyers.

The Federal Republic of Germany

Since 1935, the German Rechtsanwalt has maintained a statutory monopoly as to legal counseling and representation before the courts and administrative bodies in the Federal Republic of Germany. German citizenship is not a requirement for becoming a Rechtsanwalt, but certain education and examination requirements impose an indirect and not insignificant barrier to non-Germans. Admission to practice requires successful completion of two examinations, each involving a six-hour oral portion and either a nine-day written portion or a written portion of three or four days plus a take-home portion of four to six weeks. After the candidate has completed study at a university for a minimum of three-and-a-half to five years, the First State Examination (Referendarexamen) is administered over a period of six months to a year. The candidate (Referendar) then engages in two-and-a-half years of practical training, followed by the Second State Examination (Assessorexamen), also administered over six months to one year. The entire process takes from seven to nine years. Some of the German states have introduced an alternative system of education for admission to the Bar, whereby the candidate must pass only one final examination, after having completed a five-and-a-half year course of studies consisting of a combination of university courses and practical education.

A major exception to the statutory monopoly of the German Bar is the provision for licensed legal consultants (Rechtsbeistände). There is no citizenship requirement for obtaining a license, and the applicant must show only professional competence and good character. A Rechtsbeistand may advise clients and act as a legal consultant within the district where he is admitted, subject to the limitations specified by the chief judge of the district court (Landgericht) of the location where the applicant intends to become established. An American attorney who obtained such a license might be restricted to advising on matters of international law or American law. The extent to which he would be permitted to advise on matters involving German law is unclear.

Consultants' licenses are subject to revocation for noncompliance with the regulations governing their use, for a year's failure to use the license, or for any reason which would have justified refusal of the license had it been known at the time of application.

Even without qualifying as a Rechtsanwalt or a Rechtsbeistand, an American attorney may conduct negotiations or consultations in Germany on behalf of foreign or domestic clients, so long as such activity occurs in the ordinary course of the attorney's regular domestic practice based outside Germany. In addition, an American lawyer or law student may be employed by German lawyers with the approval of the local bar association.

Hong Kong

The legal profession in Hong Kong is modeled on the English and is divided between solicitors and barristers. In general, solicitors and barristers in Hong Kong perform the same functions as in England. Admission to the legal profession is controlled by the Supreme Court of Hong Kong under the Legal Practitioners Ordinance.

Solicitors must either be British subjects or have been ordinarily resident in Hong Kong for not less than seven years. In general, solicitors must have some university education, although neither a university degree nor a legal education or legal degree is required. Applicants who have not obtained a Post-Graduate Certificate in Laws from the University of Hong Kong must pass comprehensive legal examinations given by The Law Society of England and Wales and serve a clerkship with a practicing solicitor in Hong Kong for a period ranging from eighteen months to five years, depending on the applicant's level of education. Solicitors admitted in the United Kingdom are entitled to admission as solicitors in Hong Kong without regard to these requirements. All of these requirements, except for one examination, are also waived for barristers admitted in the United Kingdom with at least five years experience who seek to practice as solicitors in Hong Kong.[1]

While there is no requirement that persons admitted to practice as barristers in Hong Kong be British subjects, they must either have

---

[1] Legal Practitioners Ordinance §§ 3-4; Students Rules §§ 3, 6, 14-16, 20 and Second Schedule [Rule 6].

been resident in Hong Kong for eight consecutive months prior to their application for admission or otherwise satisfy the Supreme Court that they intend to be ordinarily resident in Hong Kong. In general, barristers must hold a Post-Graduate Certificate in Laws from the University of Hong Kong, and, unless they are Chinese residents of Hong Kong or have resided in Hong Kong for seven years, an LL.B. degree from that university. Applicants must also serve a one-year clerkship with a practicing barrister. Barristers qualified in the United Kingdom may be called to the Hong Kong Bar without regard to these educational requirements.[2]

As in England, the monopoly reserved to solicitors and barristers in Hong Kong is narrow. Activities reserved to solicitors and barristers include the right to prepare and issue papers in connection with court proceedings, transfers of land, and probate, and the right to represent others before the courts.[3]

Although advising on either Hong Kong or foreign law does not constitute unauthorized practice under the Legal Practitioners Ordinance, substantial restrictions on the activities of foreign lawyers are imposed as a condition to their obtaining the necessary governmental consents to reside and work in Hong Kong.

---

[2] Legal Practitioners Ordinance § 27; Barristers (Qualification) Rules § 9.

[3] Legal Practitioners Ordinance §§ 44-48.

The Director of Immigration grants the necessary consents to foreign lawyers only upon the recommendation of The Law Society of Hong Kong, which is composed of all admitted solicitors in Hong Kong and has certain disciplinary powers under the Legal Practitioners Ordinance. The Law Society has published lengthy guidelines for foreign lawyers who wish to practice in Hong Kong.[4] Applications are accepted only from foreign law firms seeking to open branch offices, not from individual lawyers. The guidelines provide a limit of two firms from any country, unless the applicant presents "evidence of a very substantial demand" for advice on its country's laws.[5] Ten United States law firms had established branch offices in Hong Kong as of May 1984.

The Law Society will only approve applications from long-established firms with substantial reputations. It will not approve the establishment of branches "to provide tax evasion or avoidance facilities for residents of the foreign country."[6] All the partners of the firm must approve the establishment of the Hong Kong office and must undertake joint and several liability for all the debts and liabilities of the branch office. The Law Society also requires details on the qualifications of the partners and other lawyers who will be resident in Hong Kong. The

---

[4] The Law Society of Hong Kong, Foreign Law Firms Establishing Themselves in Hong Kong: Guidelines to Applicants.

[5] Id. at ¶ 2.

[6] Id. at ¶ 4(b).

resident partner must be a full partner of the firm and reside in Hong Kong for at least 180 days each year.

Restrictions on the practice of foreign lawyers are set forth in the guidelines and in an undertaking which The Law Society requires from each firm applying to open a branch office in Hong Kong. First, the firm must agree to provide its services both to members of the public and to solicitors practicing in Hong Kong. Second, the firm must agree to abide both by the rules of professional ethics applicable to Hong Kong solicitors and by the rules of its home country. For example, foreign lawyers must observe the ethical rule prohibiting Hong Kong solicitors from advertising. Third, The Law Society must approve the letterhead of the firm's Hong Kong office. The firm's stationery must state the nature of the firm's qualifications, e.g., "American Counsellors at Law." Fourth, firms that intend to handle clients' funds must agree to abide by the Solicitors Accounts Rules. Fifth, the firm must agree not to "handle cases or matters unconnected with the laws of their country of origin."[7] The specific form of undertaking required by The Law Society states that the Hong Kong office will not "advise clients upon or handle directly or indirectly any matters other than those which are expected to be subject to the Federal or State laws of (e.g., the United States, the Republic of Liberia, or the Republic of Panama) (as the case may be) or

[7] Id. at ¶ 4(j).

matters which involve private or public international law or conflict of laws."[8]

The undertaking also permits The Law Society to examine the Hong Kong office's files, books and records and to ask such questions as it may determine about the firm's Hong Kong practice. However, communications between a client and a foreign legal advisor are entitled to the same privilege of confidentiality as communications between a solicitor and his client,[9] and thus The Law Society can only require disclosure of those materials and information that are not covered by the attorney-client privilege.[10]

The guidelines are inapplicable to solicitors or barristers from the United Kingdom. In general, they may practice in Hong Kong only

---

8 Form of Undertaking Addressed to The Law Society of Hong Kong at ¶ 10(a).

9 Re Duncan, Garfield v. Fay [1968] P. 306, [1968] 2 All E.R. 395.

10 While the above discussion of the role and attitudes of The Law Society of Hong Kong is thought to be accurate, there have been indications that the Attorney General of Hong Kong takes a broader view than The Law Society toward the admission of foreign law firms to practice and the areas in which they should be entitled to practice. Therefore, in certain circumstances after The Law Society has acted, the Attorney General's office may be prepared to grant the necessary immigration consents even if The Law Society has denied an application. It is believed that, in the opinion of the Attorney General, the only three conditions to be imposed on a foreign firm seeking to open a Hong Kong office are: (1) the firm must not invade the monopoly reserved to barristers and solicitors under the Legal Practitioners Ordinance; (2) foreign lawyers are prohibited from holding themselves out as Hong Kong lawyers; and (3) foreign lawyers must observe the professional rules of ethics applicable to Hong Kong lawyers.

by qualifying as solicitors or barristers in Hong Kong. At present, a number of English solicitors firms have established branch offices in Hong Kong staffed both by lawyers transferred from England who become admitted in Hong Kong and by lawyers admitted in Hong Kong originally. These branch offices are sometimes in the form of associations or other cooperative arrangements with Hong Kong-based firms. The two largest firms of solicitors in Hong Kong, for example, maintain such relationships with London-based firms.[11]

---

[11] Thomas, "The Leading Euromarket Law Firms in Hong Kong and Singapore," Int'l Fin. L. Rev. 4, 7 (June 1983).

Israel

The practice of law in Israel is restricted to members of the Israeli Chamber of Advocates, a professional body organized under the Chamber of Advocates Law of 1960 (the "Advocates Law") for the purpose of regulating the legal profession. Membership in the Chamber of Advocates is limited to Israeli "residents" and is necessary in order to benefit from the monopoly granted by the Advocates Law to licensed advocates to "practice law," defined to include not only the right to represent clients before courts and regulatory bodies, but also the right of "drawing up for another person . . . documents of a legal character" and "giving legal advice or a legal opinion." It is unclear whether the Advocates Law prohibits a foreign lawyer from giving advice in Israel with respect to foreign law, but reason suggests that it should not. Similarly, it would appear that the Advocates Law does not prevent foreign attorneys from being present in Israel to negotiate particular contracts or other legal arrangements. It is clear, nonetheless, that membership in the Chamber of Advocates is required of foreign lawyers seeking to establish themselves in Israel on a regular basis.

Generally, membership in the Chamber of Advocates is open to persons who (1) are Israeli residents, (2) have a higher legal education, (3) have served a qualifying period of legal clerkship and (4) have passed the qualifying examinations. The term "Israeli resident" is not defined for purposes of the Advocates Law, but it is clear that an Israeli advocate need not be an Israeli citizen, and the Chamber of Advocates includes many members who are "temporary residents," as opposed to "permanent residents," of Israel. In practice, unless the Chamber of Advocates has information to the contrary, the statement of an applicant that he is an Israeli resident is rarely questioned. However, Israeli advocates who move abroad for extended periods may forfeit their membership in the Chamber of Advocates.

Graduates of U.S. law schools are almost always regarded as possessing the requisite "higher legal education" required for membership in the Chamber of Advocates. Foreign law school graduates having no practical experience are required to serve a legal clerkship for two years, but the Chamber of Advocates will readily reduce this period to as little as six months in the case of foreign lawyers who have practiced abroad.

Foreign lawyers who have practiced abroad for at least two years may begin their legal clerkship before taking any of the law examinations other than for the Hebrew language examination. Applicants who can prove sufficient knowledge of Hebrew will be exempted from the language examination. The law examinations for foreign attorneys are given in eight sessions over a two-and-a-half week period. Because substantial areas of Israeli law follow patterns of common law, lawyers trained in the United States are routinely exempted from the examinations in torts, criminal law (other than procedure), corporate law and commercial law (other than taxation). The examinations are comprehensive in scope but are not regarded as being difficult, and are successfully passed by the large majority of applicants. The language of the law examinations is

Hebrew, although proctors are available and occasionally capable of assisting in translation, and answers may be written in English. It should be pointed out, however, that the law examinations aside, the achievement of at least a modest level of proficiency in Hebrew is important for successful practice in Israel.

Applicants who have practiced abroad for less than five years are in addition required to take an oral examination at the end of the period of qualifying clerkship on certain "practical" subjects, particularly procedure.

The Chamber of Advocates and the Israeli legal profession are very encouraging of foreign lawyers seeking to qualify in Israel. The Chamber organizes review courses to prepare foreign applicants for the law examinations and generally facilitates their applications. Advocates born and trained in the United States and other English-speaking countries are prominent in all aspects of the Israeli legal profession, and there is an informal network of such advocates who are ready to assist in the professional integration of foreign lawyers in Israel.

Italy

The organized legal profession in Italy, comprising *procuratori* and *avvocati*, has a monopoly as to all legal services in Italy. Membership in the profession is restricted to Italian citizens, although this restriction probably is not applicable to nationals of the European Community. There is no provision for a category resembling the legal consultant or the *conseil juridique*, but employment of foreign lawyers by Italian lawyers is permitted.

The scope of the legal services monopoly in Italy is, however, unclear in that a certain amount of counseling activities by persons not inscribed in the professional register has been authorized by court decisions.[1] While these decisions seem to permit only "occasional" non-forensic legal activities, regular and continuing non-forensic activity by foreign lawyers is tolerated in practice. There are in Italy established branch offices of foreign law firms providing general legal services other than forensic activities. These branch offices are normally staffed both by Italian and foreign lawyers. As to American attorneys, such branch offices offering non-forensic professional services apparently are permitted under the 1951 Agreement Supplementing the Treaty of Friendship, Commerce, and Navigation between the United States and Italy, which provides for rendering "technical and administrative" services to American enterprises in Italy.[2] As to lawyers from other Member States of the European Community, they are authorized to perform both forensic and non-forensic activities in Italy on a temporary basis by virtue of the European Community Directive of March 22, 1977.[3]

Japan

In the 1930's, foreign lawyers established in Japan could be licensed as *bengoshi* (attorneys) who were authorized to carry on the professional activities of *bengoshi* "in regard to aliens or foreign law as long as there is a guaranty of reciprocity"[1] (meaning reciprocity between Japan and a given foreign lawyer's country of origin). From 1949 until 1955, foreign lawyers established in Japan were eligible to qualify as *bengoshi* and become members of bar associations under a similar statutory provision (Article 7) in the Japanese Lawyers' Law as enacted in 1949;[2] this provision did not include any requirement of reciprocity. In 1955, this provision in the Japanese Lawyers' Law was repealed, and only the foreign lawyers who had theretofore been licensed under it as *bengoshi* were permitted to enjoy its benefits.[3] Thenceforth, all other foreign lawyers did not enjoy any such benefits.

Since 1955, only a very few non-Japanese applicants have gained admission to the Japanese Legal Training and Research Institute, which is a prerequisite to admission to the Japanese Bar. Also since 1955, with only one or two exceptions, non-Japanese law firms have been unable to obtain authorization to establish offices in Japan. The best-

---

[1] Law No. 53 (1933).

[2] Law No. 205 (1949).

[3] Law No. 155 (1955).

known exception was authorized by the Japanese Ministry of Justice in July 1977 but was opposed by the Japan Federation of Bar Associations ("JFBA"), and until now has not served as a precedent for the opening of other offices.

On the other hand, since 1955, individual non-Japanese lawyers have been permitted to establish themselves in Japan (a) as inside house counsel of corporations, and (b) as "trainees" or foreign legal consultants employed by Japanese law firms and companies. A significant number of American lawyers (and to a lesser extent English solicitors) are currently employed as such "trainees" or foreign legal consultants in Tokyo by Japanese law firms; and the JFBA has specifically approved the employment of foreign lawyers as "trainees" in Japan, but has not expressly approved their employment as foreign legal consultants. In addition, over the years a substantial number of foreign lawyers have received visas authorizing them to visit Japan for short periods of time on professional business.

Certain provisions in the current Japanese Lawyers' Law (Article 72) and the Japan-U.S. Treaty of Friendship, Commerce and Navigation (Article VIII) (the "Treaty")[4] have been variously interpreted with regard to the rights of American law firms seeking to establish offices in

---

[4] [1953] 4 U.S.T. 2063, T.I.A.S. No. 2863.

Japan. One Japanese authority has interpreted the current Lawyers' Law as follows:[5]

> a foreigner may freely engage in all legal affairs concerning foreign law and those legal affairs involving Japanese law that do not amount to a case as long as he does not thereby contravene some other professional statute such as the Patent Attorneys Law or the Tax Attorneys Law [footnotes omitted].

This same authority also gives a liberal construction to the Treaty, but adds, in construing the Lawyers' Law in light of the Treaty:[6]

> foreign lawyers may not go so far as to engage in the external activities of concluding a contract [as distinguished from preparing "the proposed draft of a contract"] or performing procedures in a court or an administrative agency as the authorized agent of an American national or company.

The JFBA takes a far narrower view of the Lawyers' Law and the Treaty. According to Standards issued by the JFBA in 1972, a non-Japanese lawyer acting independently in Japan must become a member of the Japanese Bar in order to draft agreements, to express legal opinions, or to meet with a client for purposes of legal consultation. The JFBA is an independent, autonomous organization which grants membership in and exercises jurisdiction over the Japanese Bar. The JFBA has received conflicting views on the question of whether foreign law firms should be permitted to establish offices in Japan. Some of its members have dis-

---

5 Fukuhara, "The Status of Foreign Lawyers in Japan," 1973 _The Japanese Annual of International Law_ (No. 17) 21, at 32-33.

6 _Id._ at 35.

missed as "pure sophistry" the arguments advanced for licensing foreign lawyers to establish Japanese offices in order to advise on non-Japanese law, and have been outspoken to the effect that foreign law firms threaten Japanese lawyers with loss of business and unemployment.[7] Other Japanese lawyers have argued that "there exists a strong demand for foreign lawyers among the foreign nationals and enterprises which have ventured into Japan."[8] In any event, as mentioned above, non-Japanese law firms have in recent years been unable to obtain authorization to establish offices in Japan.

The United States Government has indicated support for American law firms seeking to open offices in Japan, and has requested the Japanese Government to consider favorable action to this end. (Similar requests reportedly have been made by the British and German Governments on behalf of lawyers from their respective countries.) The JFBA itself has been studying the regulation of foreign lawyers outside Japan, and has become familiar with the relevant rules in (among other jurisdictions) England, France, Germany, Hong Kong and New York State. On May 20, 1984, the following article appeared on page 1 of the Japan Economic Journal (Nihon Keizai Shimbun):

---

7 E.g., Toyama, "On the Problem of Foreign Lawyers," Jurist No. 55 (1980).

8 E.g., Kosugi, "Should the Activities of Foreign Lawyers be Prohibited?," Hanrei Times No. 348 (1978).

"The Japan Federation of Bar Associations (President Seiichi Ishii) has announced that it has decided to adopt a policy of conditional acceptance of activities of foreign lawyers in Japan, which has become one of the sources of trade friction between Japan and the United States.

"The conditions are as follows:

1. The activities will exclude appearances in court.

2. The rendering of advice will be limited to foreign law and will exclude advice with respect to Japanese law.

3. The license will be for activity as a 'foreign legal consultant' and such consultants will not be permitted to employ Japanese attorneys.

4. The Federation will have jurisdiction to issue licenses.

"The Federation will soon begin internal discussions as to the precise content of the conditions.

"The Federation gave as its reasons for adoption of the new policy the fact that [Japanese] business enterprises have been increasingly active overseas and in connection with their international transactions have felt the need for international legal services, and these should be available on the basis of international reciprocity. In addition, demands from the United States to open the Japanese market for introduction of foreign legal services have strengthened and this issue has become important symbolically. Therefore, the

Federation has decided that it would be in its long-term interest to resolve this problem on its own initiative.

"In order for activities by foreign lawyers to be acceptable to Japanese attorneys, and not impinge on Japanese attorneys' activities, it is important that conditions be attached, according to the Federation. The principal thrust of these conditions would be to create a new category of 'foreign legal consultant' and to prevent foreign legal consultants from automatically doing whatever they are doing in their own countries. Also, the Federation believes that licenses should only be issued for a fixed period of time, such as two or three years, and should be renewable, if necessary. There should also be restrictions on Japanese citizens who have not qualified as attorneys in Japan but who have studied abroad and been admitted to the Bar of a foreign country.

"At the present time, the Japanese Lawyers' Law prohibits anyone who is not a member of the Japanese Bar from acting as an attorney and, therefore, foreign attorneys' activities and foreign law offices in Japan are currently prohibited. Because of this, Japanese enterprises, in connection with their overseas activities, cannot use foreign lawyers as legal advisers in Japan if they are not admitted to the Japanese Bar.

"In the near future, the Federation will prepare a draft of legislation in the form of an amendment to the Lawyers' Law, such legislation to be introduced by way of a private member's bill, as was the case with the Lawyers' Law itself."

It is understood that this proposal and questions relating to carrying it out are currently the subject of discussion between the JFBA and the Japanese Ministry of Justice.

Mexico

Opportunities in Mexico for the practice of law by non-Mexican citizens are strictly limited, both by professional licensing laws and by immigration requirements. The number of non-Mexicans admitted to practice in Mexico is small, and Mexico does not generally permit even limited practice on the basis of a lawyer's admission under the laws of a foreign jurisdiction.

The licensing of lawyers is constitutionally delegated to the governments of the thirty-two Mexican states and the Federal District (Mexico City and environs), whose laws in this matter are similar. Admission in one jurisdiction is tantamount to admission in the others. Under the Federal Law of Professions,[1] which governs the Federal District and applies to practice in matters of federal jurisdiction throughout the Republic, practice of the profession of law (ejercicio profesional) requires a degree (título profesional de licenciado en derecho), awarded by a recognized institution, and the acceptance thereof for registration by the appropriate authorities, which in turn issue a license (cédula profesional) to practice.[2]

---

[1] Ley Regulamentaria de los Articulos IV y V Constitucionales, relativos al -- ejercicio de los Profesiones en el Distrito y Territorios, Articles 2 and 8, as amended.

[2] Practice of law is defined as the habitual carrying out or rendering, whether or not for consideration, of any acts or services characteristic of the legal profession, or in any other manner holding oneself out as a professional lawyer.

Although Articles 1 and 33 of the Mexican Constitution extend civil rights (garantias) to foreigners as well as to nationals, the Law of Professions requires that, in order to practice, a lawyer must be a citizen of Mexico. (Very few foreigners are granted Mexican citizenship.) On the other hand, the Supreme Court of Mexico has established that, in requiring citizenship for the practice of law, the Law of Professions violates Article 5 of the Constitution, which guarantees that no person may be denied the right to engage in the profession, industry, trade or work that he chooses, so long as it is legal. Under Mexican constitutional law, however, the Court's holding of unconstitutionality has not repealed or rendered ineffective the offending provision of the Law of Professions; each aggrieved person must bring a constitutional action (juicio de amparo) for the application of the Court's established constitutional holdings (jurisprudencia)[3] to his own case. Furthermore, admission of foreigners by an amparo also requires fulfillment of Mexico's educational requirements, and thus foreigners who have obtained law degrees elsewhere must "revalidate" their degrees in Mexico, a process usually requiring supplementary studies there. It is believed that most foreigners licensed to practice in Mexico are from Latin America and that many of them have been educated wholly or substantially in Mexico.

---

[3] Suprema Corte de Justicia, tesis número 1925, Amparo en Revisión. 3847/1959, Manuel de Jesús Padilla, 3 de mayo de 1960, Mayo Ediciones 1966-1970, Tomo II at 466-7.

The immigration laws also limit the practice of foreigners in Mexico. For example, admission to the Bar even by amparo as mentioned above is available only to permanent residents (inmigrados), an immigration status requiring at least five years' prior legal residency as an immigrant (inmigrante). Inmigrante status is accorded to foreign professionals only in "exceptional cases" and even then only after registration of their foreign degrees.[4] The immigration laws do not provide explicitly for non-Mexicans licensed abroad to enter even temporarily for the practice of law. Otherwise, foreigners with degrees from other countries may be admitted only to teach in special fields approved by the authorities, to act as consultants or instructors in the organization of educational or scientific institutions or laboratories, or to serve as technical directors in the exploitation of certain natural resources, subject always to the conditions imposed by the Federal Government and the terms of the visas issued by the immigration authorities. Applications for immigration and temporary visas must be filed by the Mexican employer of the proposed immigrant, and are granted infrequently.

In addition to the Laws of Professions and of Immigration, the Law for the Control and Registration of the Transfer of Technology and the Use and Exploitation of Patents and Trademarks of 1982 requires, under severe penalties, approval and registration by the Technology Registry of contracts providing for the performance in Mexico by foreigners

---

[4] Immigration Law (Ley General de Población), Article 48(III).

of advisory or consultative services for Mexicans, unless the services contract is to be in effect for no more than two months in a period of a year, in which case the contract only need be filed of record, not approved. Some officials of the Technology Registry have expressed the opinion that this provision applies to foreign professionals, including lawyers. However, so far as can be determined, no contracts for legal services had been recorded or filed through December 31, 1983.

Article 147 of the Income Tax Law taxes at a rate of 30% income from fees for services, including legal services, that may be performed in Mexico. A Mexican client is required to withhold the tax from the gross amount at the source.

The Netherlands

The practice of law in The Netherlands is divided into three regulated professions: (1) advocaten, the legal advisors to a party in litigation; (2) procureurs, to whom practice before Dutch courts is reserved by law; and (3) notarissen, semi-public officials with exclusive authority to effect certain transactions (such as the creation of bodies corporate and the conveyancing of real property). The professions of advocaat and procureur are governed by the Advocatenwet[1] which requires that an advocaat or a procureur have passed the doctoral examination in Dutch law at one of the recognized Dutch universities and that he or she be a member of the Bar of one of the court-districts.[2] In practice the distinction between the two professions has virtually disappeared since almost all advocaten are also procureurs and carry both titles. There is a single Bar for both professions. A member of the Bar must complete a three-year stage with an experienced member of the Bar. Dutch citizenship, or citizenship of a European Community Member State, is not required for admission to the Bar.

While procureurs have a legal monopoly on representation before the courts, neither they nor advocaten have a monopoly on the rendering of legal advice. Anyone, whether Dutch or foreign, and regardless of

---

1 Advocatenwet of June 23, 1952, Staatsblad 365.

2 Members of the Bar of The Hague are also admitted to practice before the Supreme Court (Hoge Raad).

whether he or she has had any legal education, can render legal advice and use a title such as "juridisch adviseur (raadgever)" (legal advisor or consultant). The profession of legal consultant is not formally organized or subject to legal regulation.

A national of a country outside the European Community who wishes to become established in The Netherlands as an advocaat, procureur or legal consultant must obtain a residence authorization and a work permit. To obtain a work permit, such a national must persuade the authorities that his or her activities will not adversely affect employment by Dutch or EC nationals, and usually must show that he or she will establish a relationship with a Dutch law firm.

The Orde van Advocaten (a semi-public institution which has legislative and judicial powers over advocaten and procureurs)[3] has issued a regulation concerning cooperation between Dutch advocaten and foreign lawyers.[4] Pursuant to this regulation, a Dutch advocaat can enter into partnership with a foreign lawyer having a permanent residence in The Netherlands if the latter (1) has practised for at least three years in the foreign jurisdiction in which admitted to practice and (2) submits to the rules of professional conduct of the Orde.

---

[3] Article 134 of the Dutch Constitution.

[4] Verordening No. 8 (Samenwerkingsverordening) of November 24, 1972, effective January 1, 1973 (Staatscourant 1972, No. 252).

Notarissen have their own, separate professional organization (*Koninklijke Notariële Broederschap*). A member of the Bar may also be a *notaris*.

Nigeria

Nigeria is a federal republic consisting of 19 states whose rules of practice and procedure are locally determined.[1] Regulation of the legal profession, however, is centrally administered and admission to practice in any state entitles a lawyer to practice anywhere in Nigeria. Entry into the legal profession and the general regulation of lawyers are governed by Decree Number 15 of May 15, 1975 (the "Legal Practitioners Decree"). Regulations pursuant to the Legal Practitioners Decree are promulgated by the Attorney General of the Federal Republic, who must first consult with the executive committee ("Bar Council") of the Nigerian Bar Association.[2]

Authorization to practice in Nigeria is limited to individuals falling into one of three categories: (1) an individual who has been registered on the Roll of the Supreme Court of Nigeria, pursuant to the rules of that Court; (2) an individual who, upon application by him or on his behalf, has been authorized by the Chief Justice of the Federal Republic to practice in respect of a specific proceeding; or (3) an individual in the public service of the federal or a state government who has been authorized to practice law because the discharge of his duties as a public servant requires him to do so.[3]

---

[1] [1979] Constitution of the Federal Republic of Nigeria § 239.

[2] Legal Practitioners Decree §§ 1, 6(2).

[3] *Id.* § 2.

Registration on the Roll of the Supreme Court is generally open only to members of the Nigerian Bar.[4] Admission to the Bar is limited to Nigerian citizens[5] who have completed the requisite legal training. Such training includes the completion of a three-year undergraduate program in law in Nigeria or abroad, followed by a year of study at a Nigerian law school. Under certain circumstances, foreign lawyers may seek registration on the Roll of the Supreme Court.[6] The Attorney General of the Federal Republic, after consultation with the Bar Council, "may by regulation provide for the enrollment of the names of persons who are authorized by law to practice as members of the legal profession in any country where, in his opinion, persons whose names are on the Roll are afforded special facilities for practicing as members of that profession." The Legal Practitioners Decree also empowers the Attorney General to prescribe the terms and conditions, if any, under which such foreign lawyers may be registered on the Roll.[7] The Attorney General is empowered to revoke any such enrollment with respect to lawyers whose native countries do not afford to Nigerians special facilities to practice law.[8] Because the Attorney General has not yet promulgated any rules to imple-

---

[4] Id. § 6(1).

[5] As defined in §§ 23-28 of the 1979 Constitution of the Federal Republic of Nigeria.

[6] Id. § 6(2).

[7] Id.

[8] Id. § 6(3).

ment these provisions of the Legal Practitioners Decree, no foreign lawyers have yet been registered on the Roll of the Supreme Court pursuant to its terms.

The Chief Justice of the Federal Republic may grant the application of an individual to practice law in respect of a specific proceeding if such individual "appear[s] to him to be entitled to practice as an advocate in any country where the legal system is similar to that of Nigeria."[9] Such permission extends to all actions related to the specified proceeding, including appeals and many collateral actions. This provision seems to be intended to cover foreign lawyers, although it is not so limited by its terms.

An Attorney General, a Solicitor General or a Director of Public Prosecutions, whether in a state or in the federal government, may engage in the practice of law in connection with the discharge of his duties. Furthermore, any individual in the service of the federal government or the government of any state may practice law if the Attorney General of the relevant government specifies by order that the discharge of the duties of such public official requires that he be permitted to practice law. Such an order may relate generally to the office or be limited to a particular individual.[10]

It should be noted that the Legal Practitioners Decree regulates only the actual practice of law. Nonqualified foreign lawyers are thus

---

[9] Id. § 2(2).

[10] Id. § 6(3).

prohibited from appearing before courts and other tribunals that make legally enforceable rulings, decisions and orders, and from the paid preparation of legal documents. However, a foreign lawyer with the requisite visa is not prohibited from acting as a consultant with respect to legal matters, and at least one foreign lawyer has in fact acted as a legal consultant in Nigeria. Moreover, the Legal Practitioners Decree explicitly recognizes this distinction in excepting from its coverage an individual who acts as an "expert" in preparing documents for the benefit of someone else.

Singapore

Admission to the Singapore Bar is open to any person, regardless of citizenship, who satisfies the educational and practical-experience requirements under the Legal Profession Act. The basic educational requirement is satisfied by an LL.B. degree from Singapore University, or alternatively, by admission as a solicitor or barrister in England. Further educational requirements include a three-month Post-Graduate Practical Course in Law offered by the Singapore Board of Legal Education, followed by a comprehensive legal examination. The practical-experience requirement consists of a six-month clerkship with a practicing attorney of seven years' standing at the Bar. The Singapore Bar is unified, recognizing no distinction between solicitors and barristers, and admitted attorneys are entitled to plead in any Singapore court.

Foreign lawyers seeking to practice in Singapore must apply to the Attorney General, who has complete discretionary authority over their admission to practice. His authority is not specifically set forth by statute, but the Singapore immigration authorities will not issue the necessary work permits without his consent. Although the Attorney General has not issued written guidelines on his policies toward foreign lawyers, his office will respond to individual requests for information.

No foreign law firms were permitted to open offices in the Republic of Singapore until the early 1970's, when the Attorney General permitted several American law firms to open offices there on a trial basis. In 1974, however, all but one of these offices were asked to close, and no other foreign law firms were permitted to practice in Singapore until 1979, when the Attorney General adopted the current policy of granting entry to selected foreign law firms. At least eighteen foreign law firms now have offices in Singapore, including firms from the United States, England, Australia, The Netherlands and Indonesia. Although Singapore law firms are not allowed to share profits with foreign firms, several local firms have some form of association with foreign firms.[1]

Under present policies, applicants must be reputable law firms with an international practice. The application to the Attorney General must describe the firm's proposed areas of specialization in Singapore, the Singapore office's proposed staff, and their qualifications. Foreign law firms permitted to open offices in Singapore are allocated a specific number of work permits, which may be increased on application to and approval by the Attorney General. In addition to approving applications by foreign law firms to open Singapore offices, the Attorney General reviews applications for the entry of each foreign lawyer proposed to staff such offices.

The Attorney General requires that the Singapore office of a foreign law firm limit its practice to advice in connection with offshore transactions. Foreign law firms must submit periodic reports summarizing their work to demonstrate compliance with this requirement. Foreign

---

1 Thomas, "The Leading Euromarket Law Firms in Hong Kong and Singapore," Int'l Fin. L. Rev. 4-7 (June 1983).

firms are generally not permitted to practice or advise on Singapore law, although the Attorney General has permitted one firm of English solicitors to maintain a local practice by admitting two of its solicitors to the Singapore Bar.[2]

---

[2] Id. at 7.

Rules of the European Community

The Commission of the European Community has been engaged for some years in preparing rules to govern the exercise of professional activities in one Member State of the European Community ("EC") by a lawyer from another Member State.[1] One long-pending EC Directive would deal with the right of lawyers in one Member State to establish themselves as lawyers in other Member States. As a result of differences between the legal systems and professional traditions in the various Member States, however, progress in connection with the right of establishment has thus far been slow,[2] and adoption of an EC "establishment" Directive does not seem imminent.

An existing EC Directive concerns the right of lawyers from one Member State to render services in other Member States. An early draft Directive on this topic was withdrawn for revision following a 1974 decision by the European Court of Justice in the Reyners case[3] to the effect

---

1 The EC Member States are Belgium, Denmark, France, Germany (Fed. Rep.), Greece, Ireland, Italy, Luxembourg, Netherlands, United Kingdom.

2 See Brunois, "Le Barreau et la libération des prestations des services et des établissements dans la communauté economique européenne," Revue Européenne, pp. 398-434 (1977); Leach, "EEC: Moves towards a Directive on Freedom of Establishment for Lawyers in the European Community," Law Society's Gazette (London, June 25, 1980).

3 Reyners v. Belgium, European Ct. Justice Case No. 2/74 (June 21, 1974), [1974 Transfer Binder] Comm. Mkt. Rep. (CCH) ¶ 8256. See also van Binsbergen v. Bestuur, European Ct. Justice Case No. 33/74 (Dec. 3, 1974), [1975 Transfer Binder] Comm. Mkt. Rep. (CCH) ¶ 8282.

that the Treaty establishing the European Economic Community (the Treaty of Rome)[4] forbids a host Member State to discriminate on grounds of nationality in regulating activities of a lawyer from another Member State.

On March 22, 1977 the European Council of Ministers adopted a Directive "to facilitate the effective exercise by lawyers of freedom to provide services."[5] Under this Directive the Member States are required to adopt the national legislation necessary to carry it into effect, and the deadline for enacting this legislation was March 22, 1979. Four of the Member States met this deadline; they are Denmark, France, Ireland and the United Kingdom.[6] Five other Member States, Belgium, Germany, Italy, Luxembourg and The Netherlands, have since enacted the required legislation.[7] Only Greece (which became a member as of January 1, 1981) has not as yet completed enactment.

---

4 [1977] 298 U.N.T.S. 11.

5 European Community, Council Directive No. 77/249 to facilitate the effective exercise by lawyers of freedom to provide services, O.J. Eur. Comm. (No. L 78) 17 (March 22, 1977), Comm. Mkt. Rep. (CCH) ¶ 1494.

6 Denmark, Law No. 93 of March 14, 1979, and Ministry of Justice official communication No. 94 of March 15, 1979. France, Decree No. 79-233 of March 22, 1979. Ireland, Statutory Instrument No. 58 of 1979, European Communities (Freedom to Provide Services) (Lawyers) Regulations, Feb. 27, 1979. United Kingdom, The European Communities (Services of Lawyers) Order in Council, 1978 No. 1910; Dec. 20, 1978, effective March 1, 1979.

7 Belgium, Law of December 2, 1982, and Royal Decree of March 14, 1983. Germany (Fed. Rep.), Law of August 16, 1980. Italy, Law No. 31 of February 9, 1982. Luxembourg, Law of April 29, 1980. The Netherlands, Law of October 15, 1980.

The Directive requires each host Member State to recognize lawyers who are admitted to practice in other Member States and who render legal services in the host State. It requires such lawyers to use the same professional titles used by them in the Member States from which they come.[8] "Activities relating to the representation of a client in legal proceedings or before public authorities shall be pursued in each host Member State under the conditions [with certain exceptions] laid down for lawyers established in that State . . . A lawyer pursuing other activities" shall be governed by the rules of professional conduct of the Member State from which the lawyer comes, "without prejudice to respect for" the host Member State's fundamental rules of professional conduct.[9]

Lawyers covered by the Directive are the members of the Bars of the various Member States as well as, in the case of the United Kingdom and Ireland, solicitors. The Directive does not mention lawyers from non-Member States. Since it deals with the "occasional" rendering of legal services by foreign lawyers and not with the permanent offices of foreign law firms, the Directive should not directly affect American law firms having offices in Europe.

---

[8] Comm. Mkt. Rep. (CCH) ¶ 1494, Art. 3.

[9] Id., Article 4. See generally, Mauro, "L'application de la directive du 22 mars 1977 [etc.]," Gazette du Palais 1979. I. Doctr. at 322 (Paris, June 16, 1979). For a comparative study of the legislative texts enacted by nine Member States see Laguette, "Textes pris par les Etats de la C.E.E. pour l'Application de la Directive du Conseil des Communautés Européennes Concernant la Libre Prestation de Service des Avocats," Gazette du Palais 1984 (Paris, Jan. 8-10, 1984 at 2 and Jan. 11 & 12, 1984 at 2).

Selected Bibliography

American Bar Association & National Conference of Bar Examiners, Joint Conference on Bar Admissions of Foreign Law School Graduates (D. Boshkoff ed. 1976).

Bassiouni, "Licensing of Foreign Legal Consultants in Illinois: A Report," 64 Ill. B.J. 580 (1976).

Boshkoff, "Access to State Bar Examinations for Foreign-Trained Law School Graduates," 6 Hofstra L. Rev. 807 (1978).

W. Boulton, Conduct and Etiquette at the Bar (6th ed.) (London 1975).

Brothwood, "International Law Offices," 1979 J. Bus. L. 8 (1979).

Brunois, "Le Barreau et la libération des prestations des services et des établissements dans la communauté economique européenne." Revue Européenne (1977).

Busch, "The Right of United States Lawyers to Practice Abroad" (pts. 1-3), 3 Int'l Law. 297, 617, 903 (1969).

Campbell & Coe, Transnational Legal Practice: A Survey of Selected Countries (D. Campbell ed. 1982).

M. Cappelletti, J. H. Merryman & J. M. Perillo, The Italian Legal System (1967).

E. J. Cohn, Manual of German Law, vol. 1 (2d ed. 1968).

Commant, "Foreign Practice - Problems and Developments," 73 Int'l B.J. 59 (1973).

Cone, "Foreign Lawyers in France and New York," 9 Int'l Law. 465 (1975).

The Council of the Law Society, A Guide to the Professional Conduct of Solicitors (London 1974).

I. S. Forrester & H. Ilgen, The German Legal System (1972).

Fukuhara, "The Status of Foreign Lawyers in Japan," 1973 The Japanese Annual of International Law (No. 17) 21.

S. K. Huber, "Admission to the Practice of Law in Texas: A Critique of Current Standards and Procedures," 17 Hous. L. Rev. 687 (1980).

Jeantet, "Cooperation with a French Avocat - Private Investors Abroad," Prof. and Solutions in Int'l Bus. 187 (1974).

Knoppke-Wetzel, "Employment Restrictions and the Practice of Law by Aliens in the United States and Abroad," 1974 Duke L. J. 871 (1974).

Kosugui, "Regulation of Practice by Foreign Lawyers," 27 Am. J. Comp. L. 678 (1979).

Kosugui, "Should the Activities of Foreign Lawyers be Prohibited?," Hanrei Times No. 348 (1978).

Leach, "EEC Moves Towards a Directive on Freedom of Establishment for Lawyers in the European Community," Law Society's Gazette (London, June 25, 1980).

J. Lemaire, Les Règles de la Profession d'Avocat et les Usages du Barreau de Paris (Paris 1975).

Levy, "The American Lawyer in Paris," 52 N.Y. St. B.A.J. 647 (1980).

Lund, Sir Thomas, "Problems and Developments in Foreign Practice," 59 A.B.A.J. 1153 (1973).

Note, "Foreign Attorneys: The Right to Practice," 8 J. of Legal Prof. 209 (1983).

Note, "Foreign Branches of Law Firms: The Development of Lawyers Equipped to Handle International Practice", 80 Harv. L. Rev. 1284 (1967).

Note, "The Practice of Law by Out-of-State Attorneys," 20 Vand. L. Rev. 1276 (1967).

Note, "Providing Legal Services in Foreign Countries: Making Room for the American Attorney," 83 Colum. L. Rev. 1767 (1983).

A. Nyssens, Introduction à la Vie du Barreau (2d ed.) (Brussels 1974).

L. M. Roth, "Requirements for American Lawyers to Practice Law in Israel," 15 Int'l Law. 433 (1981).

Salter, "Transnational Business and International Lawyers," 73 Com. L. J. 69 (1968).

Thomas, "The Leading Euromarket Law Firms in Hong Kong and Singapore," Int'l Fin. L. Rev. (June 1983).

D. C. Thompson, How to Become a Lawyer in Canada (Edmonton 1979).

Toyama, "On the Problem of Foreign Lawyers," Jurist, No. 55 (1980).

R. Trouillat, Les Conseils Juridiques (Paris 1979).

D. C. Turack, "Access to the State Bar Examination for Foreign Trained Graduates: The Ohio Experience," 8 Ohio N.U.L. Rev. 265 (April 1981).

Walker, "Reforming Inter-State and Overseas Admission Rules in Australia: A Strategy for New Zealand," New Zealand L. J. (June 1983).